WALKING MORE RIDGES OF LAKELAND

Also by Bob Allen and Peter Linney

WALKING THE RIDGES OF LAKELAND

Also by Bob Allen

ON HIG H LAKELAND FELLS
ON LOWER LAKELAND FELLS
ESCAPE TO THE DALES
ON FOOT IN SNOWDONIA
SHORT WALKS IN THE LAKE DISTRICT

Also by Peter Linney

THE OFFICIAL WAINWRIGHT GAZETTEER

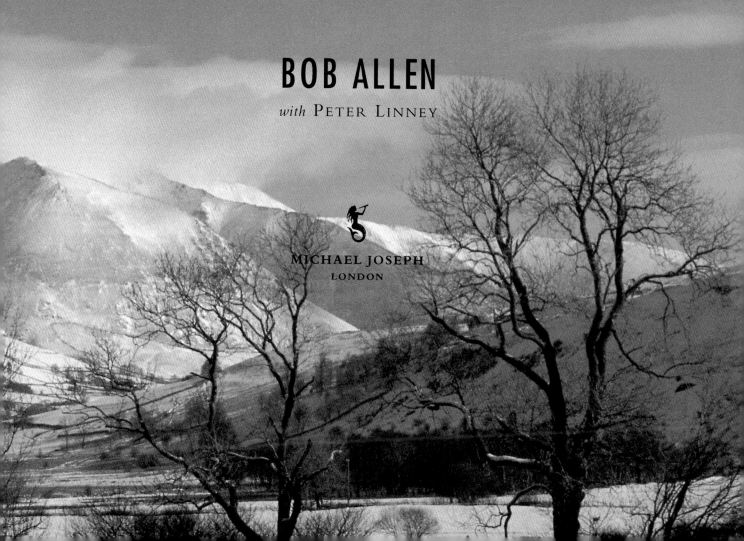

WALKING MORE RIDGES OF LAKELAND

according to WAINWRIGHT'S PICTORIAL GUIDES *Books 4–7*

BOB ALLEN

with PETER LINNEY

MICHAEL JOSEPH
LONDON

MICHAEL JOSEPH LTD

Published by the Penguin Group
27 Wrights Lane, London W8 5TZ
Viking Penguin Inc., 375 Hudson Street, New York, New York 10014, USA
Penguin Books Australia Ltd, Ringwood, Victoria, Australia
Penguin Books (NZ) Ltd, 182–190 Wairau Road, Auckland 10, New Zealand

Penguin Books Ltd, Registered Offices: Harmondsworth, Middlesex, England

First published in Great Britain 1996
1 3 5 7 9 10 8 6 4 2

Typeset by Cambridge Photosetting Services
Colour reproduction by Saxon, Norwich
Printed in Singapore by Imago

A CIP catalogue record for this book is available from the British Library

ISBN 0 7181 3930 5

The moral right of the author has been asserted

Half-title page: Great Gable seen from the north-west cairn on Lingmell
Title page: Blencathra seen from the south-west
Endpapers: Looking towards Hindscarth from Hindscarth Edge

CONTENTS

PREFACE

by PETER LINNEY

It is now over two years since I first met Bob Allen with Jenny Dereham to discuss the possibility of a book of the best walks based on the ridges noted by A. Wainwright in his seven incomparable Pictorial Guides to the Lakeland Fells. I described in the preface to the first book how the ridge-route map came about and, although I do not want to repeat myself completely, I do think a short explanation is sensible.

AW identified no fewer than 318 ridge routes between the 181 Lakeland fells which have ridge connections (33 of the 214 fells described in the seven guides have no stated connection with a neighbouring fell). I drew my first map indicating the position of the fells in 1982, and when I started gathering information for my book, *The Official Wainwright Gazetteer*, my engineering background nagged at me to look at the presentation of the information. This led me to add the 178 starting points specifically indicated or hinted at by AW in the guides, together with the ascents to the fells shown as straight dotted lines. When I came to consider the ridge routes, which AW detailed at the end of his descriptions of the relevant fells, I added these to the maps in the form of solid straight lines connecting the appropriate fells. It is this map, the relevant part of which is shown on page 11, that forms the basis of the two books of ridge walks.

The first volume (covering Books One, Two and Three of the Pictorial Guides) is already published and, in completing many of the walks described by Bob in this second volume, it has been a delight to revisit fells which were old friends, and exciting to walk routes new to me. And, despite the position in which Bob decided to photograph me as my official 'author photograph' (page 8), I promise you that I enjoyed my 'walk' up Sharp Edge!

The study of the Pictorial Guides required for my small part in these two books has reinforced my view that, despite the thirty years or so which have elapsed since AW completed the final book, *The Western Fells*, I am more and more staggered at the enormity of the task he set himself – and completed in the allotted time – and the sheer quality of the information provided in the seven guides. Yes, there are factual changes brought about by the passage of time which have to be recognised, but the fundamental 'truth' of the work remains as valid as when AW first completed his 'love letter to the fells'.

The last rise to Red Pike (Wasdale) from Scoat Fell.

INTRODUCTION

Peter Linney on Foule Crag, above Sharp Edge.

At the time of publication of the first volume, I was asked during an interview: 'Why is this book specifically about walking along *ridges*?' Most fellwalkers know instinctively why, but there are several good reasons which are worth airing. A ridge provides a natural route, often allowing views of the landscape on both of its sides; also, to climb to the top of a mountain or a fell by a ridge leading to its summit is often the safest way; and, most importantly, it provides a sense of exhilaration which is at its greatest when steep ground drops away on either hand. The narrowest ridges give a little frisson of excitement that can never be felt when simply walking over flat ground.

The glorious English Lake District is rightly famed for the large number of 'horse-shoes' or 'rounds' that can be devised for walking over its fells, connecting felltops by linking ridges. Alfred Wainwright (who is referred to hereafter in this book as AW) obviously knew this. In the seven volumes of his superlative Pictorial Guides to the Lakeland Fells he ended each chapter by giving directions to the next felltop by a ridge route, where one was applicable. Peter Linney then turned those into a diagrammatic map showing how the felltops are linked together and that map, as it applied to AW's Pictorial Guides 4, 5, 6 and 7, is the basis of this book – *see* page 11. But there are actually more ridges in Lakeland than appear on this map, for example The Band to Bowfell, or the other Band to Great End. So wherever possible I have made use of these also so that the walks not only use the connecting ridges between felltops but also ascend to the first top by way of a ridge and descend from the last top also by means of a ridge.

This second book deals with the Southern Fells, the Northern Fells, the North Western Fells and the Western Fells, and because the *first* volume ended with Part Three, this *second* volume begins with Part Four. I have had room for 27 ridge walks; for the last walk I have added two 'Wainwright tops' to turn what would otherwise have been a short ridge into a great day's walking. In consequence all walks end back where they started. In those four Pictorial Guides, AW described ascents to 116 tops. The 27 walks I have described and illustrated cover 88 of them with very little overlapping, more than 76% of the total; many of the 28 not covered are isolated outliers. The walks cover in all just under 270 miles of glorious fellwalking, with a total height gain of nearly 94,000ft. The average is 10 miles, with a height gain of 3480ft; all should give a satisfying day's fellwalking.

I must specifically mention one great horseshoe walk which I have not included: the Ennerdale Skyline. It shows up clearly on the ridge-line map and it is indeed a walk which I have myself done several times. But, and it is a very big but, its successful completion, covering all the tops in the circuit, involves over 9000ft of ascent and almost 28 miles of distance. It would take the average fellwalker between 13-15 hours (although very fit and fast walkers or fellrunners will reduce that, of course). But I decided that this is too much of a marathon for the vast majority of fellwalkers and that I could cover all the relevant Wainwright tops, and all the ridges, in more manageable sections.

Several of the walks in this volume (and specifically Walks 6, 7 and 8) involve traversing the Scafell massif, the highest and roughest ground in England. The connections between Scafell Pike and Scafell, in both directions, are not obvious or easy. Erosion, by weather and booted traffic, has made some routes between them much more unsafe than they used to be. On the other hand, a major improvement to the Foxes Tarn path as a result of work by the National Trust has made that route much better than formerly. I do therefore urge all newcomers to fellwalking on the Scafell massif (and old-timers who may not have visited it for some years) to use the linking routes recommended in the text.

MAPS: Because of the variations in the length and shape of walks and the necessity to fit them to the page size of the book, the maps are inevitably at different scales, but I hope that they will prove helpful and illuminating nonetheless. The red pecks indicate the described and recommended route. That does not always mean that there is necessarily a path on the ground, although there usually will be. When I mention the 'main path' in the text, that is an abbreviation for 'the most used and obvious path *on the ground*', which is not always the same as the path indicated on the Ordnance Survey map. Extra care needs to be taken in summer when tall bracken may sometimes obscure paths or turns, and in winter when deep snow may obliterate them entirely.

GRADIENT PROFILES: Their purpose, and the scale of them, is to try to give the most realistic idea of what the particular slope *feels* like when you are doing it.

ROUTE CARDS/TABLES: The heights listed are in feet as used by AW, the foot anyway being a natural unit of measurement which this author (or his editor) is not prepared to abandon to European standardisation. Unfortunately the Ordnance Survey caved in some time ago and so modern maps are metric; furthermore some heights have been revised since AW wrote his guides. The metric heights given may therefore not necessarily convert to AW's figures in feet; the metric ones used are those found on the latest OS 1:25 000 maps, or an estimate where no specific height is given.

PLACE NAMES: These are those generally used by the Ordnance Survey, although a few of the older spellings, which AW preferred (as does this author and his editor) have been retained. A specific difference is that AW insisted on using Eel Crag instead of Crag Hill.

Bob Allen on the ridge between Broad Crag and Scafell Pike.

TIMES: The times given for completion of any of the walks are a guide only, based on a consideration of AW's times, Naismith's Rule (three miles per hour plus half an hour per thousand feet of ascent) and the times I personally managed while doing the walks. They do allow for a few short stops but not for long ones.

ACCESS: Fellwalkers in the Lake District enjoy an almost unrestricted freedom to roam on the high land above the level of the intake walls. This is a very valuable freedom and must be safeguarded by all walkers behaving responsibly, in particular by only using public rights of way (or permissive paths where rights of way are not shown on the OS maps) to reach the high land, and ensuring that all gates are closed after use. I have taken great care to ensure that all routes described in this book do not infringe this principle, making slight modifications to AW's routes where necessary. Compass directions are often given in the text and it should be obvious that a compass and the correct map or maps should always be carried.

ACKNOWLEDGEMENTS

The older I get the more grateful I become for the splendid Ordnance Survey maps and I must acknowledge that debt here. Peter Linney's splendid work in producing the Wainwright ridge-line network is where this project began and the book would not have been created without him. But he has also been responsible for the gradient profiles and the route cards and tables, while his son Andrew has done the graphic work necessary and rendered my maps legible.

My editor, Jenny Dereham, has, as always, worked like a demon to get all the bits in the right places, remove the inconsistencies, polish the presentation: she's a treasure. The direct quotations from the Pictorial Guides to the Lake District are reproduced by kind permission of Michael Joseph Ltd. The area managers of the Lake District National Park have been, as always, enormously helpful in sorting out access problems, while the excellent work on footpaths being done by the National Trust – which deserves every walker's support – has greatly improved some of the conditions underfoot.

On the fells, my wife, Lin, has managed a few walks (things are looking up), while Peter Linney, Harry Sales, Roger Bowers, Trevor Waller and Elsa Fieldhouse have all given me welcome support. I thank them all. Sadly my little canine pal Freddie, who has accompanied me on the walking for all my books, died just before this one was completed: Henry, my other dog, is still going strong. By the time this book is published, Freddie the Second will surely be part of the family.

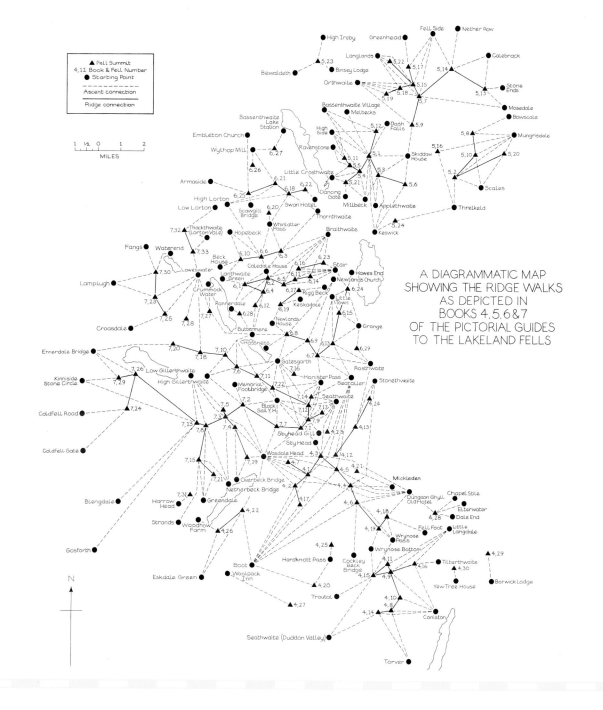

A DIAGRAMMATIC MAP
SHOWING THE RIDGE WALKS
AS DEPICTED IN
BOOKS 4, 5, 6 & 7
OF THE PICTORIAL GUIDES
TO THE LAKELAND FELLS

▲ Fell Summit
4,12 Book & Fell Number
● Starting Point
------- Ascent connection
——— Ridge connection

1 ½ 0   1   2
MILES

N

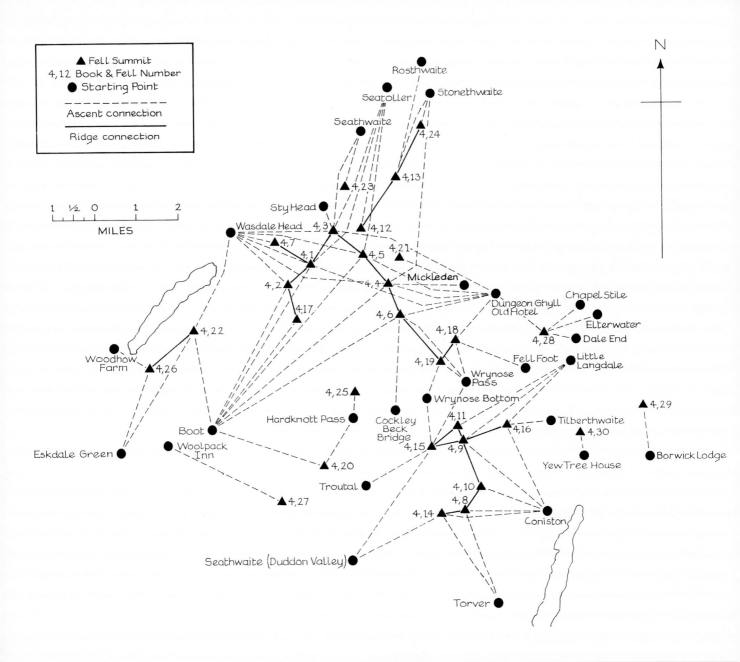

N

Rosthwaite
Seatoller
Stonethwaite
Seathwaite
4,24
4,13
Sty Head
4,23
Wasdale Head 4,3
4,12
4,7
4,21
4,1
4,5
4,2
4,4
Mickleden
4,17
4,6
Dungeon Ghyll Old Hotel
Chapel Stile
4,18
Elterwater
4,28
Dale End
4,22
4,19
Fell Foot
Little Langdale
Woodhow Farm
4,26
Wrynose Pass
4,25
Wrynose Bottom
4,29
Hardknott Pass
4,11
Tilberthwaite
4,16
4,30
Cockley Beck Bridge
4,15
4,9
Eskdale Green
Boot
Yew Tree House
Borwick Lodge
Woolpack Inn
4,20
Troutal
4,10
4,8
4,14
Coniston
4,27
Seathwaite (Duddon Valley)
Torver

▲ Fell Summit
4,12 Book & Fell Number
● Starting Point
- - - - - Ascent connection
———— Ridge connection

1 ½ 0   1   2
MILES

12

PART FOUR

THE SOUTHERN FELLS

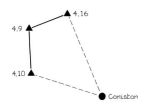

1 A CONISTON CIRCUIT FROM BRIM FELL

BEST MAP: *OS 1:25 000 Outdoor Leisure 6, South Western area*
APPROXIMATE TIME: *5¼ hours*
TERRAIN: *Good paths leading to a rougher and steeper grass and scree rake for the ascent of Brim Fell, then good paths along the rest of the main ridge.*

ITINERARY	Book & Fell No	Height of ascent	Distance of ascent	Cumulative distance	Height above sea level	
		feet	miles	miles	feet	mtrs
CONISTON					200	61
Brim Fell	4.10	2450	3.00	3.00	2611	796
Swirl How	4.09	400	1.50	4.50	2630	802
Wetherlam	4.16	500	1.25	5.75	2502	762
CONISTON			3.50	9.25	200	61
Totals of heights and distances of ascent		3350	9.25			

This particular circuit of the Coniston fells is different from what many walkers familiar with them may have come to expect, for it climbs to the main ridge by a little-used and direct ascent of Brim Fell that is worthy of much more attention than it has received so far. The remainder is classic high-level ridge-walking.

There are, thankfully, numerous parking spaces in Coniston, one being up Station Road (on the site of the old station), but all that is necessary is to park somewhere and then follow signs to the Sun Hotel, turning to the right behind it. A most pleasant path now leads forward across meadows and beneath trees up the left bank of Church Beck, passing by the stone-arched Miners Bridge and then curving left away from the ravine. It climbs bracken and grass slopes, which look across to the former copper and iron smelting sites of what was once a substantial industrial complex, then joins the broad and rough road rising to the former slate quarries on Coniston Old Man's east face. Join it, but only to leave it immediately for a level terrace on the right. This too was a quarry track, shortly

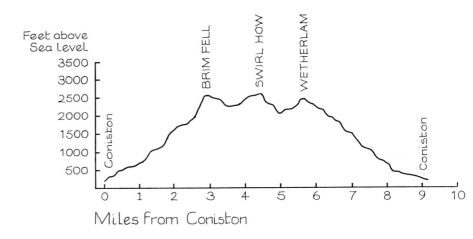

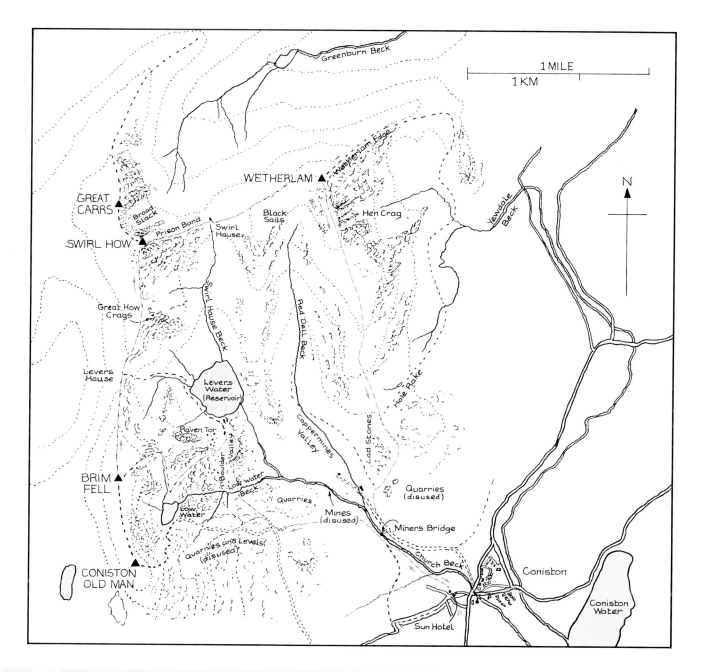

GREENBURN BECK

GREAT CARRS ▲

Broad Slack

SWIRL HOW ▲

Prison Band

Swirl Hause

WETHERLAM ▲

Wetherlam Edge

Black Sails

Hen Crag

Yewdale Beck

N

Great How Crags

Swirl Hause Beck

Red Dell Beck

Levers Hause

Levers Water (Reservoir)

Hole Rake

Raven Tor

Boulder Valley

Coppermines Valley

Lad Stones

BRIM FELL ▲

Low Water Beck

Low Water

Quarries

Quarries (disused)

Mines (disused)

Miners Bridge

Quarries and Levels (disused)

CONISTON OLD MAN ▲

Church Beck

Coniston

Sun Hotel

Coniston Water

1 MILE
1 KM

Brim Fell, sunlit above the shadowed fellside, from Church Beck.

ending on a flat area where there are two truncated towers built of slate and below some huge spoil heaps. While walking along this the route of ascent to Brim Fell can be clearly distinguished and it is worth a moment's study. Brim Fell's east ridge ends in Raven Tor, whose main crags are out of sight on the northern flank, but the southern flank clearly shows two bands of rock with an easy-angled sloping rake separating them. It is this rake which gives the route as far as Low Water.

When the quarry track ends, a footpath continues across the slope, soon passing the huge Pudding Stone and crossing Low Water Beck by a footbridge. This path continues up the right edge of the appropriately named Boulder Valley, past the belt of rocks down which Low Water Beck tumbles and splashes, but you must leave it to cross to the bottom of the rake dividing this band of rocks from the higher one, which looks now like a very compact belt of steeply angled slabs. There is a length of rusty, twisted iron pipe amongst the boulders at the bottom of the rake to confirm that it is the correct one.

The way starts up grass but then continues up what looks suspiciously like mining spoil, a conjecture confirmed beyond doubt when you find two short lengths of iron rail sticking out of the turf at the top of the rake. The rails run back into a mine driven into the depths of Brim Fell and there is even an iron trolley, abandoned many years ago and firmly rusted to the rails at the mouth of the tunnel. Just outside is what was clearly once a little hut with wooden spars and corrugated tin roof, but it is all collapsed now and disappearing under boulders shed from the crags above. It is interesting that although the hut would have been visible when it was still upright, the mouth of the adit is not easily seen from the valley below. AW called it a 'cave' on his drawing (Brim Fell 3) and, rather curiously and very unusually for him, did not mention the trolley which is rusted to the rails. Just a little further on the rake ends; it was clearly once used as a ramp or incline furnished with iron rails to transport material from the mine to the foot of Brim Fell.

A faint trod curves away from the top of the rake and soon reaches the point where Low Water Beck disappears over a lip of rocks. Low Water itself is only 150 yards ahead, backed by a cirque of crags and steep ground rising up to the main ridge linking Coniston Old Man with Brim Fell. A feeder beck drains into it from the right (north) side of the cirque and a faint path traces its course up a grass slope, then curves away from it up a groove to reach a hause. This hause separates Raven Tor from Brim Fell and a few strides up to the right leads to Raven Tor's summit. From here there is a grand view down to Levers Water and across the intervening valley to the south ridge of Wetherlam, by which this walk returns.

Turning now westwards up the slope towards Brim Fell, a faint path leads over grass and some stretches of very easy scramble-walking over lovely speckled rocks to reach the north-east cairn, in an area of grey stones; this marks the start of the descent route back to Low Water. The main summit cairn on Brim Fell is in excellent condition, a large beehive-shaped mound. It isn't a great viewpoint, as the top is too flat and extensive, but the Scafells stand out on the skyline to the north-west.

A steady descent of about 400ft leads down the slope northwards, over stones and shale and then down rather eroded grooves in the grass to Levers Hause, followed by a similar ascent up the opposite slope, on the edge of the steep drop on the right and reaching the proud rock pike of Great How Crags, often mistaken for Swirl How. On the way, a careful visual search of the boulders below Great How Crags, well seen from this vantage point, will reveal the little circular fox-bield, constructed to trap foxes, built amongst them; it is an almost perfect example.

The path that you now need to Swirl How descends very slightly from Great How Crags then rises, cutting across an earthy section and then continuing almost on the level over jumbled rocks to where they end abruptly at a steep scarp high above the Greenburn valley. Here is the fine tall cairn crowning Swirl How's summit, perched on rocks above the drop and looking across the deep scree gully of Broad Slack to Great Carrs. To stand here for a few moments, preferably in contemplation of the landscape rather than just huffing and puffing and tucking your shirt in, is to realise the truth of AW's comment that this, although not the highest, is the true 'geographical centre' of the Coniston fells.

Appropriately, Swirl How marks a sharp change of direction for this round, as Wetherlam, the last top, is to the east, detached from the main spine of the Coniston fells but connected to it by the crumpled ridge of Prison Band. This holds no problems as a well-marked path turns down it, skipping easily down rock slabs and little walls, skirting three rockier humps on their right-hand side and shortly reaching the narrow pass of Swirl Hause. A big heap of stones, a collapsed cairn, sits in the gap, but if you seek shelter for a few moments it is better to find it amongst the last rocks of the descent than on the hause itself. A footpath nowadays turns down the dry northern slope towards the Greenburn valley and another, an old miners' path used by modern walkers, starts the descent towards Coniston from here by traversing across the slope beyond towards Black Sails, but the most used path, and the one needed, goes half-left from the hause and climbs a fairly steep and rough slope to reach easier ground on the broad ridge that leads to Wetherlam.

Purists may leave the path and continue the direct climb to Black Sails, whose rough and knobbly subsidiary ridge falls towards Coniston, continuing along the highest land towards Wetherlam in the north-east, and then rightly feel superior when they reach it. But most sensible walkers will probably follow the path which takes the easiest line. This sticks closely to the left-hand edge of the high ground, overlooking the Greenburn valley, and gains little further height as it crosses peaty ground in the area of Red Dell Head Moss, then a last long rise up a stony slope leads to the rocky top of Wetherlam. It somehow always seems further than you might expect from Swirl How, no doubt because of the great bulk of the mountain, but the splendid views from the summit, particularly towards the Langdales, are ample compensation.

Head south, veering leftwards (SSE) from Wetherlam's summit, passing close to the edges of the fairly spectacular gullies that define Hen Crag and along the tops of the broken cliffs overlooking Yewdale Beck and Tilberthwaite Gill. The gentle and very pleasant descent becomes steeper towards the depression of Hole Rake and then the path swings right onto what is generally known as the Lad Stones ridge. (This, incidentally, is clearly shown on the OS inch-to-the-mile maps but not at all on the metric ones.) A few twists and turns through former slate quarries soon lead to the broad gravel track beside Church Beck and if you follow this for no more than a couple of hundred yards you will be able to turn off right and cross Miners Bridge, thus completing the circuit. A stroll beside Church Beck will then soon lead you past (?) the Sun Hotel and back to the car at Coniston.

The Yewdale Fells seen from the top of the Hen Crag gully on Wetherlam.

2 THE LOW WATER SKYLINE

BEST MAP: *OS 1:25 000 Outdoor Leisure 6, South Western area*
APPROXIMATE TIME: *4½ hours*
TERRAIN: *Sometimes indistinct grassy paths on the ascent, good paths on the summit ridge, fainter paths and grassy rakes for the descent.*

ITINERARY	Book & Fell No	Height of ascent	Distance of ascent	Cumulative distance	Height above sea level	
		feet	miles	miles	feet	mtrs
CONISTON					200	61
Coniston Old Man	4.08	2450	3.00	3.00	2633	803
Brim Fell	4.10	80	0.50	3.50	2611	796
CONISTON			3.50	7.00	200	61
Totals of heights and distances of ascent		2530	7.00			

Despite hints, suggestions and advice from guide-book writers such as AW and even myself it is fairly obvious that the vast majority of fellwalkers never in fact buy a guide-book (or do not read them if they do) for they still continue to flog their way up to the summit of Coniston Old Man by way of the signposted route through the spoilheaps of the old quarries on the east flank of the mountain. Much of that route involves slithering uphill on a rolling bed of stones and is a form of purgatory that you can cheerfully recommend to your worst enemy. The south flank route via Boo Tarn is very much better and is the one used on this circuit.

AW started from Coniston and toiled up Station Road and then up the very steep hill beyond the Sun Hotel and narrow tarmac road that follows, which is signed 'Walna Scar and Coniston Old Man'. You may do the same, if you choose, and the distances and heights given in the tables assume that you do. But most walkers nowadays prefer to park about 500ft higher and a mile further on, immediately beyond the gate at the end of the tarmac, where there is a space for about fifty cars (grid ref 289971).

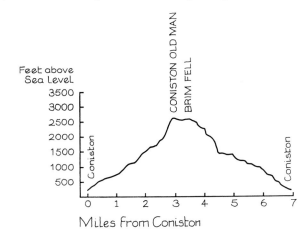

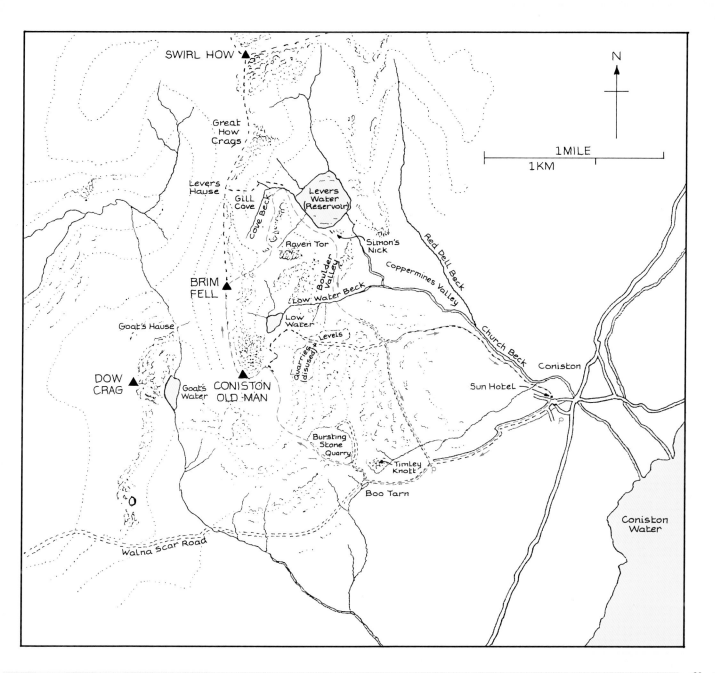

SWIRL HOW ▲

N

1MILE
1KM

Great
How
Crags

Levers
Hause

Gill
Cove

Cove Beck

Levers
Water
(Reservoir)

Red Dell Beck

Simon's
Nick

Coppermines Valley

Raven Tor

Boulder Valley

Low Water Beck

BRIM
FELL ▲

Low Water
Beck

Church Beck

Coniston

Goat's Hause

Low
Water

Levels

Coniston

DOW
CRAG ▲

Goat's
Water

Quarries (disused)

Sun Hotel

CONISTON
OLD MAN ▲

P

Bursting
Stone
Quarry

Timley
Knott

P

Boo Tarn

Coniston
Water

Walna scar Road

21

Ignoring the signposted quarry track heading off to the north, continue instead to the south-west along the Walna Scar Road, which is now just a track leading eventually over the Dow Crag ridge to the Duddon Valley. My wife (on one of her rare moments joining me on a ridge walk) walked along with a group of geology students all wearing white plastic helmets balanced on their heads. One student told me wryly that it was a legal requirement, perhaps, he suggested, in case meteorites fell from the sky. I had the distinct impression that he thought that the cult of safety and its attendant regulations were getting crazier with every passing year – as they are.

The 'road' passes by the fine little outcrop of Timley Knott and then, immediately before passing the tiny Boo Tarn, which is now so full of reeds that you may even fail to notice any water, a rough quarry track turns off uphill to the right, heading for Bursting Stone Quarry. You should leave the Walna Scar Road here, turning off right, keeping beside a tiny stream and initially just left of the quarry track. New workings at the quarry have meant that the line of ascent on AW's drawing (Coniston Old Man 7) has been changed and a cairned grassy trod now climbs uphill to the left of a quarry spoil heap. The top of the Old Man remains out of sight and faith is needed to follow this ingenious but carefully cairned path as it swings more noticeably to the left and always on the easiest grassy gradient. Not until it has slanted above the top of the quarrying area does the path turn sharp right and up a gently inclined grassy groove which becomes almost level where it overlooks the terraces of grey-green slate below. At the end of this groove the first view of Wetherlam is obtained over the Coppermines Valley. The path then zigzags back left and right on a long rising traverse across the fellside to a shoulder and junction with the last part of the east-face quarries path which I denigrated earlier. However, the summit is now near and in view and you can enjoy the fine sight of Low Water below the rough slopes of the east face without having had to eat any of the dust on the way up.

The last part of the ascent is up an obvious shoulder to reach the large circular platform of slates constructed on the top. There is usually a crowd of people scoffing crisps and sandwiches round the substantial cairn on the platform, which is higher than the nearby trig point, but with luck you will be able to touch it in the ritual manner before sidling away to find a quieter place to enjoy your own lunch. A little down the slope to the west there is still a bit of grass to sit on with a grand view across to the splendid buttresses of Dow Crag.

The main spine of the Coniston fells leads north from here and an obvious stony path now leads along the ridge, which is also the rim of the combe enclosing Low Water. It descends slightly for a quarter-mile to a point where another path veers off downslope to the left towards Goat's Hause (although Goat's Water is not yet in sight). It then rises gently to an area of stones in the middle of which is a large beehive-shaped cairn, clearly in better condition than when AW surveyed it. This marks the broad, domed top of Brim

The Scafells seen from the main cairn on Brim Fell.

Fell. Beyond, in clear conditions, the skyline is dominated by the mass of the Scafell range. About a hundred paces to the north-east is another large cairn and immediately beyond it are broken rock outcrops which lead down towards Brim Fell's east ridge. This is now the start of the descent.

There is little trace of a path but the descent is down pleasant slopes of grass and little rock ledges, very easy scramble-walking, with Levers Water visible far below and to the left of the line of the ridge. Descend to a distinct col or dip, beyond which a little lip of rocks rises again, crowned by a cairn. This col is 400ft below the top of Brim

Coniston Old Man and Low Water seen from near Raven Tor on Brim Fell.

Fell and marks the point beyond which Raven Tor begins. This is a mass of rock, sloping away steeply on its northern flank and which appears, from a distance, to be a major crag, although closer acquaintance reveals an easier than suspected angle. A stroll beyond the cairn reveals more grand views across a wide combe to Great How Crags and Swirl How.

Returning to the col, a narrow path will be found leading down left (north) across a scree slope and towards another little col directly in line of sight with the pyramid of Great How Crags beyond. From this second col, although the path fades, it is easy to follow the line of the right-hand bounding rib of rock and grass into Gill Cove. Lower down, more steep rocks make it advisable to traverse leftwards and cross Cove Beck to join the obvious cairned path seen rising from Levers Water up to Levers Hause. In its upper reaches this path is dreadfully loose and unpleasant, so take care, but its lower parts are firm enough and give a reasonable descent towards Levers Water, now seen ahead.

A good although narrow and rather stony path now leads along the south-west side of Levers Water just above water level, traversing below the extensive broken crags of Raven Tor. It passes very close to the old workings of Simon's Nick, at the south end of the reservoir, where reddish spoil heaps on either side of several stark and dramatic rifts in the earth are very evident. Fenced-off shafts and notices warn of the risk of collapsing ground and an untimely disappearance into the nether regions, so the path wisely turns very slightly uphill just to the right of the shafts and before reaching the area. A grassy col is immediately reached and the path then leads down a tongue of land on the other side, on the edge of Boulder Valley; this is named from the numerous large rocks which litter the declivity, having clearly fallen from the upper slopes of Brim Fell.

Low Water Beck, which tumbles over extensive crags higher up the slope, is crossed by a footbridge only twenty yards or so from the great detached rock known as Pudding Stone. Nearby, an iron water pipe runs back up the fellside to the enormous slate quarrytips above, a reminder of the extensive industrial past of this valley in mining and quarrying. From the Pudding Stone and on the same level you can look back towards Brim Fell, about a hundred yards beyond Low Water Beck, and see the circular tunnel of an adit, with a beautifully built arched entrance, that was driven into the guts of the mountain. I don't think we would have enjoyed walking here when water was sloshing down those great pipes and the bowels were being visibly dug out of the fellsides.

Shortly after leaving the Pudding Stone, the footpath joins a good track at the foot of some huge tips on a flat area where the remains of two slate pillars suggest that there was once an incline or cableway. This then contours round a rock outcrop colonised by juniper and immediately reaches the old quarry road heading up the Old Man (and battered into dust by the feet of those legions of pilgrims on the 'direct' east-face quarries route). If you started from Coniston you will turn left downhill here and simply follow the footpath slanting across the fellside and then down beside Church Beck past the Sun Hotel for the return. If you parked at the higher level at the end of the Walna Scar Road you should also turn left downhill here, but then immediately right (south) and this good former quarry road simply traverses below the fellside and back to the car park at the end of the tarmac section of the Walna Scar Road.

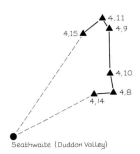

Seathwaite (Duddon Valley)

3 THE SEATHWAITE TARN ROUND

BEST MAP: *OS 1:25 000 Outdoor Leisure 6, South Western area*
APPROXIMATE TIME: *6¼ hours*
TERRAIN: *A firm track leading to rougher ground and faint paths on the ascent, then good paths are joined for the continuation and the descent.*

ITINERARY	Book & Fell No	Height of ascent	Distance of ascent	Cumulative distance	Height above sea level	
		feet	miles	miles	feet	mtrs
SEATHWAITE (Duddon Valley)					350	107
Grey Friar	4.15	2200	4.00	4.00	2536	773
Great Carrs	4.11	300	0.88	4.88	2575	785
Swirl How	4.09	130	0.33	5.21	2630	802
Brim Fell	4.10	380	1.50	6.71	2611	796
Coniston Old Man	4.08	100	0.50	7.21	2633	803
Dow Crag	4.14	425	1.00	8.21	2555	778
SEATHWAITE			3.75	11.96	350	107
Totals of heights and distances of ascent		3535	11.96			

Seen from the beautiful Duddon Valley, where this walk begins, the day ahead and the tops along the ridges to be traversed on this round may look innocuous, uninteresting or even boring. However, the initial impression is misleading for these apparently gentle slopes conceal a deep combe, a seldom visited place of peace and quiet. There will be no hordes crowding your footsteps here. And 'boring' is the last word you will think of when you reach the main ridge and peer over it to view the dramatic ice-scoured landscape beyond.

Parking facilities are very limited at the hamlet of Seathwaite in the Duddon Valley and it is probably better to park just beyond the point where the tarmac of the Walna Scar Road ends. For this, drive half a mile north of Seathwaite to where the road crosses Tarn Beck at Seathwaite Bridge; then, immediately before reaching the bridge, turn off right onto a single-track tarmac lane signed 'Coniston, unfit for cars.' Keep right and continue as far as a gate, parking on the verge just beyond it but before reaching another gate 100 yards further on (grid ref 239968).

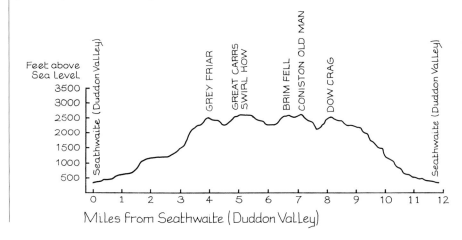

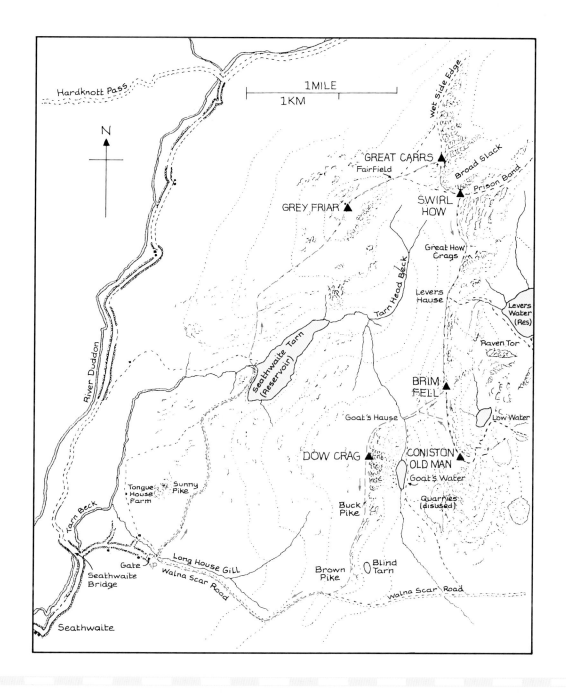

Hardknott Pass

1 MILE
1 KM

N

GREAT CARRS ▲
Fairfield

Wet Side Edge

Broad Slack

Prison Band

GREY FRIAR ▲

SWIRL
HOW ▲

Great How
Crags

Tarn Head Beck

Levers
Hause

Levers
Water
(Res)

River Duddon

Seathwaite Tarn
(Reservoir)

Raven Tor

BRIM
FELL ▲

Low Water

Goat's Hause

DOW CRAG ▲

CONISTON
OLD MAN ▲

Tongue
House
Farm

Sunny
Pike

Goat's Water

Buck
Pike

Quarries
(disused)

Tarn Beck

Long House Gill

Brown
Pike

Blind
Tarn

Gate

Walna Scar Road

Walna Scar Road

Seathwaite
Bridge

Seathwaite

The bouldery track of the Walna Scar Road leads ahead up the line of Long House Gill and will be used on the descent so now turn left and climb the iron ladder-stile beside the upper gate. The gravelly track beyond is the waterwork's access for Seathwaite Tarn Reservoir and it slants across open fellside, almost immediately allowing views to Harter Fell and the Scafells, with Ill Crag for once looking like a separate mountain instead of just a pimple on the shoulder of Scafell Pike. Close at hand are the rough crags of Sunny Pike and below them the intricate mosaic of stone walls and green fields surrounding Tongue House Farm, the result of centuries of patient cultivation.

After an easy mile, the track runs out onto the level and swings right (north-east), with the dark line of the top of the reservoir appearing ahead and quickly reached. The slopes of the south-west ridge of Grey Friar stretch beyond the dark waters, slopes supported by some steep crags, with four or five separate buttresses being distinguishable and all overlooking the flat moss at the head of the tarn. These are marked as a single large buttress, unnamed, on the OS map, whereas AW shows crags named 'Great Blake Rigg' on his drawing (Grey Friar 6). The route to be followed slants to the right and above but well left of them.

Large paving stones have been laid around the parapet of the dam, enabling you to promenade along it as if at Blackpool, although nobody is selling ice cream, and a steel-mesh footway (reminiscent of those films shot in multi-storey prisons) leads across the overflow from the dam and the feeder for Tarn Beck. These strike a fairly incongruous note but are soon forgotten as you single out one of several easy-angled grassy gullies, all trending rightwards towards the crest of the south-west ridge. Leaving the dam and then crossing some boggy ground to the north, the chosen gully or grass groove beyond soon leads to drier slopes, giving easy going. About 500 feet above the tarn, the grassy crest of the ridge is reached and you are able to see beyond it to Mosedale, to Hardknott Pass and to upper Eskdale. A faint path soon appears, leading gently upwards, picking a way between a few scattered boulders and passing by a cairn on a sharp rock outcrop over on the right. More small boulders soon appear and then there is the sparkle of white quartz amidst a plateau of grey rocks and you have reached Grey Friar.

There are two rock outcrops on the summit, about forty yards apart and each sports a cairn. The higher of the two is clearly that to the south-east, which AW illustrated, while that to the north-west certainly commands the better view, directly up Mosedale. AW suggested that you would need 'a simple 20' rock climb' to reach the north-west cairn, but this would only be true if you were attempting to reach it by coming straight up the steep slope from Cockley Beck in the Duddon Valley. Normally you would just walk from the south-east cairn over grass and stones onto a slightly tilted slab of rock, then reach the cairn in barely one step of 2ft or less.

You may feel reluctant to leave Grey Friar, which is so peaceful and relatively un-trodden, but the main ridge beckons now, with Great Carrs the next objective. Seen

Seathwaite Tarn backed by Brim Fell; the ridge to Grey Friar is on the left.

from Grey Friar, Great Carrs appears to have little individuality and certainly no character, looking like a simple grassy mound with a few grey stones on its slopes and two cairns on its top. An easy-angled slope leads to the north-east towards it, running out onto a broad grassy hause. This is called Fairfield but bears no resemblance whatsoever to the fine mountain of the same name in the eastern fells. Then, although the OS map clearly shows a right-of-way path leading directly up the easy slope beyond to the top of Great Carrs, there is no path on the ground. The two paths which are there curve off on either side, one towards Wet Side Edge and the other towards Swirl How, so you must stroll up trackless grass to Great Carrs.

When I came this way last, the conditions were rather hazy, with low cloud swirling around in a sinister manner. As I climbed, I became aware of the silhouette of a cross on the skyline ahead and of several rounded shapes next to it, looking remarkably like gravestones. Nearer to, these suddenly resolved into long-skirted Herdwick sheep which stamped their feet rudely at me and then drifted away. The cross stands upright in a cairn of stones built on some bits of the wreckage of a Halifax bomber which crashed here on 22 October 1944. Somebody has obviously been in touch with the MoD, as a typewritten letter and a list in a plastic cover (which will not survive long up here) has been placed amongst the stones. This advised that the aircraft was based at RAF Topcliffe and was used for training crews to operate the Halifax bombers. At the time of the accident, the crew, seven of whom were Canadian and one a Brit (from Scotland), were on a nightnavigation exercise. If the plane had had only another 20 feet of height and gained 50 yards' distance it would have cleared the ridge ahead.

Turning left up the last bit of slope, the main cairn on Great Carrs is soon reached and found to crown a surprisingly steep and extensive rock buttress stretching towards the valley of the Greenburn Beck far below. It commands a tremendous view and your arrival here will be a moment to savour. Then, descending slightly and following round the rim of the deep combe of Broad Slack, a similar short rise climbs to the particularly fine cairn on the next top, Swirl How. This marks the junction of two ridges, that of Prison Band coming from Wetherlam via Swirl Hause and that which you will now be following to the south, along the main spine of the Coniston fells.

The path is cairned over rocky ground for a short way, then cuts an obvious blaze across a grassy section before rising to the proud outcrop of Great How Crags. From here you can look out over Levers Water and across to the boldly tilted and rust-tinted crags of Raven Tor on the east ridge of Brim Fell, which remains in sharp outline on the descent that follows to Levers Hause. On the right, you will have a full-length view of Seathwaite Tarn and will be able to pick out a couple of small grey spoil heaps, relics of former mining operations, near its head.

A steady climb follows up Brim Fell, with the path a wide blaze on the earth in the lower parts but becoming less clear, although excessively cairned, on the stonier ground near to the top. The beehive-shaped cairn marking it is so well built and so large that a close relative of mine (who shall remain nameless) was able to attend to a brief call of nature behind it without anyone else being aware of the fact.

The stony path continues along the ridge to Coniston Old Man, with a slight descent and then rise to the large platform with its cairn and nearby trig point. Strictly, you should go to the summit and if you never have been there you must certainly go. On the way over you will see where an obvious path slants down north-eastwards to Goat's Hause and can pick it up after your summit visit. If, however, the usual crowd of people are swarming all over the top of the Old Man, I'm sure you will be forgiven for turning off

at the cairn on Brim Fell and heading WSW down grassy slopes and directly towards Goat's Hause and the splendid Dow Crag buttresses, soon seen to be soaring upwards from extensive red and grey scree slopes lapped by Goat's Water.

A spring wells up on this slope of Brim Fell and the waters flow to the hause itself, giving a welcome chance for a drink, before they diverge, with a trickle going down each flank, some to Goat's Water, some to Seathwaite Tarn. Thereafter an obvious rocky path up the edge beyond leads to an easy scramble onto the summit of Dow Crag, one of the finest in the Lakes, where three little fangs of rock surmount a greater mass of rock overlooking the great crags below. Anyone wishing to avoid the scramble would be well advised to go round to the right: going left could lead to a sudden plop into Goat's Water. About 100 yards south of the summit, the path passes the heads of Great Gully and then Easy Gully, both giving spectacular views into the depths, before continuing on grass and rising to rocks on Buck Pike. A further gentle decline follows, with Blind Tarn suddenly coming into view below, then a last short rise takes you to Brown Pike, where there is a good cairn and windbreak amongst many flat stones.

This is not the end of the ridge, but it is as far as AW's ridge-line map takes us, and it is the most convenient place from which to return to the Duddon Valley. The Walna Scar Road, here a good gravelly path, is quickly reached at a grassy col by turning south-west down the short slope from Brown Pike, and it then slants across the fellside before turning more steeply downhill beside Long House Gill to reach the car again.

Looking back to Grey Friar from Swirl How, with Broad Slack on the right.

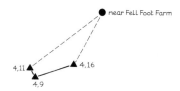

4 THE GREENBURN BECK ROUND

BEST MAP: *OS 1:25 000 Outdoor Leisure 6, South Western area*
APPROXIMATE TIME: *5 hours*
TERRAIN: *Faint paths and boggy bits in the early stages and final return; on clear and frequently rocky paths on the main ridges.*

ITINERARY	Book & Fell No	Height of ascent	Distance of ascent	Cumulative distance	Height above sea level	
		feet	miles	miles	feet	mtrs
Near FELL FOOT FARM					400	122
Wetherlam	4.16	2400	3.00	3.00	2502	762
Swirl How	4.09	620	1.25	4.25	2630	802
Great Carrs	4.11	75	0.33	4.58	2575	785
Near FELL FOOT FARM				4.00	8.58	400	122
Totals of heights and distances of ascent		3095	8.58			

The combe drained by the Greenburn Beck has the fine tops of Wetherlam, Swirl How and Great Carrs at its head and this walk is a very satisfying circuit of those tops, going clockwise along the ridges which enclose it to the north-east.

There could be access problems with Wainwright's suggested routes of ascent to Wetherlam or to Great Carrs. His ascent to Wetherlam from Little Langdale village via Low Fell takes in the whole of the long north-east ridge, and might be useful if you are actually staying there or being dropped off there. But his route over Low Fell is not straightforward and your chances of parking a car in Little Langdale village are virtually nil. On an anti-clockwise circuit, his suggested ascent to Great Carrs from Fell Foot Farm involves crossing intake walls, requiring permission from the farmer, which might under-

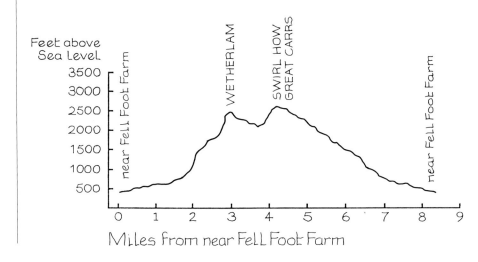

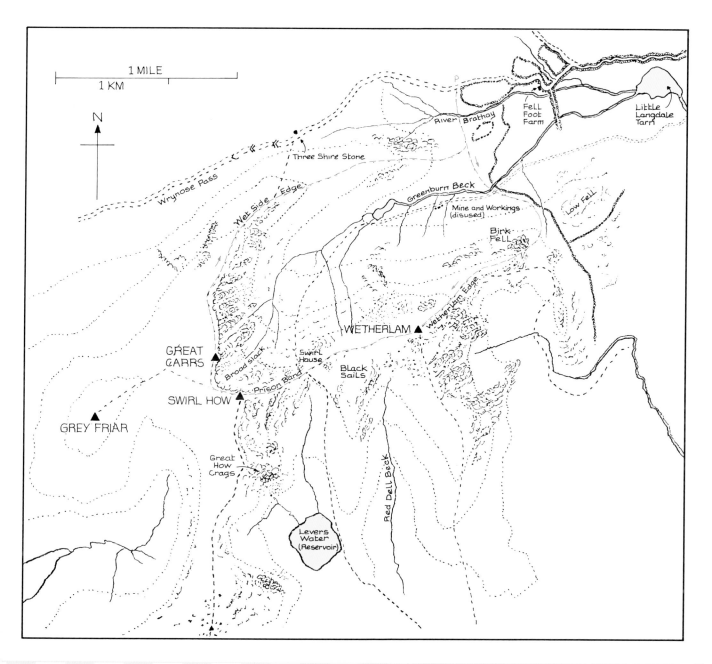

1 MILE
1 KM

N

Wrynose Pass

Three Shire Stone

Wet Side Edge

River Brathay

P

Fell Foot Farm

Little Langdale Tarn

Greenburn Beck

Mine and Workings (disused)

Birk Fell

Low Fell

WETHERLAM ▲

Wetherlam Edge

GREAT CARRS ▲

Broad Slack

Swirl House

Black Sails

SWIRL HOW ▲

Prison Band

GREY FRIAR ▲

Great How Crags

Levers Water (Reservoir)

Red Dell Beck

standably be refused, nor can you park there. My suggested route is, therefore, a variation on AW's and involves crossing the grain of the land a little, but you should certainly find a parking place and you don't have to cross any walls. Are there *any* snags? There are two streams to cross, in both directions, but they are well furnished with good boulders and it is extremely unlikely that they will present any difficulties.

A good place to park is at the bottom of the Wrynose Pass (linking Little Langdale with the Duddon Valley) on its eastern side, about half a mile west of Fell Foot Farm. To be precise, the tarmac road going west up to the Wrynose Pass takes a right-angle turn immediately after passing the farm and has a wall on its left-hand side. Drive on until just before the intake wall on the left apparently comes to an end (in fact, it turns sharp left). There is a public footpath sign on this corner pointing to the right – in the opposite direction, in fact, of the walk. The right-hand side of the road is unenclosed (allowing a grand view of the Langdale Pikes to the north-west) and it is possible to park half a dozen cars on the grassy verge here (grid ref 293032). The wall turns south down the slope towards the beck, the River Brathay. What looks like a tractor track leads towards the stream, but it soon fades so choose your own crossing point to ford the waters. Climb the grassy slope opposite, keeping right of the almost circular wall surrounding a bit of sloping fellside, onto the big toe of the ridge ahead. This is the ridge running down from Great Carrs via Wet Side Edge and the one which will be used for the return journey, but it is necessary to cross it in order to reach the far ridge of the combe for the ascent to Wetherlam.

Just over the ridge you will see another intake wall and should trend right to keep outside it and descend a short but steep grassy slope to where Greenburn Beck splashes through some pleasant little gorges. Boulders here provide the means of crossing dryshod to the southern bank to reach a good track marching up the valley; this formerly served the disused Greenburn copper mines. Cross this also and climb the slope beyond, heading roughly south-east and shadowing a wall. The OS map shows green pecks marking paths which were originally in daily use by the copper miners, but they are now hardly walked at all, so you will see few traces until you are above them and higher up the slope. The fellside above has extensive rocky ground and is tangled with junipers so it is best to stay close to the wall on the left, until you go over a rise and into a shallow subsidiary valley, at a point where a ladder-stile crosses the wall. Here swing right (SSW), crossing one of the old miners' paths which becomes briefly visible, and follow the bank of a small beck below some prominent broken crags on Birk Fell.

Veer more to the south-west as the ground becomes rougher and steeper and you will soon be picking a zigzag way up grassy ledges and a few rock shelves and climbing onto Birk Fell itself. As the angle eases a path appears – although, from the lack of a path below, it looks very likely that it has been formed by walkers who have descended from Wetherlam, strayed off the normal path, found themselves at the top of this steeper ground

Looking down Wetherlam Edge to Birk Fell, with Little Langdale Tarn.

at the end of Birk Fell, dithered and then retreated. This path now leads the way forward, over the superbly rough and largely flat rocks along the top of Birk Fell, where there are numerous quartz outcrops. There are fine views to the Langdale Pikes to the north.

A very slight descent to a hause follows, just before the ascent to Wetherlam by way of Wetherlam Edge. This resembles the tilted corner of a house, with a long wall stretching away to the left. The path begins by going to the right of a couple of large rock slabs and continues up easier rock onto the ridge itself. There are now several paths rising up the ridge, but they all follow the same general line, climbing up sloping grooves and a few shattered rock walls, then up easy-angled rock shelves and more grooves through some tiers of flat rock to reach a rocky and fairly level summit area. It is an enjoyable ascent, reaching a fine top which, because it projects from the main ridge of the Coniston fells, gives some grand views, particularly towards Little Langdale. In windy conditions, however, it is fairly inhospitable as there is really only one good place to shelter, behind the rock supporting the main summit cairn.

Because of the stony ground, paths off the summit are not very obvious, particularly under snow, but the general direction of the path needed towards Swirl Hause is a little south of west. It is cairned, but not very obviously so, and it may help in poor conditions to realise that it does not go along the broad top of the ridge towards the rising hump of

Black Sails, but steers a course lower down on the right than might be expected, along the edge of the broad top overlooking the head of Greenburn. It then reaches some fairly rough ground and there is a steeper descent to negotiate to Swirl Hause. Even when I've been here in winter, with the wind tearing through the gap, making my eyes water and my nose run continually, I have always found other walkers huddled here, seeking inadequate shelter behind the big pile of stones.

The ridge rising beyond the hause is known as Prison Band. In the cirque of rough ground stretching from it towards Levers Water are the broken rocks of Prison Crag, and also an area called The Prison, situated just below Great How Crags. There is, in fact, a prison there, a sloping-sided trap for foxes, known as a fox-bield, built of stones, very old and a wonderfully preserved example of its kind. The path up Prison Band is obvious, rising past three rocky humps but keeping left on the steepest ground. It is an entertaining and not too arduous climb, allowing good views down to Levers Water and culminating in a fine tall cairn on Swirl How, the second top. The best views are to the north and north-east.

A deep wide gully, Broad Slack (which I had better not get the wrong way round), separates Swirl How from the third top, Great Carrs, which is in full view across the semi-circular head of the gully to the north-west. A simple descent curving round the rim and then rising leads in only a few minutes to a main cairn (for there is another) perched on rocks at the head of a surprisingly steep rock buttress overlooking great depths into the Greenburn valley. The rock face of which this buttress is the most striking feature is seamed by deep gullies and forms a dramatic termination to the easy-angled grass slopes on the western side. It is a pity that the rocks are too shattered to tempt the rock climber, but competent scramblers will find at least one route of interest here.

In walking round the top of Broad Slack and up to Great Carrs, you may well spot a cross in a pile of stones just fifty yards down the western slope. This marks the few remains of a Halifax bomber which crashed into the slope in October 1944 while on night-flight training. The further remnants of torn metal, spotted down in the combe below Broad Slack, show clearly that it must have only just failed to clear the top of the ridge.

The obvious descent to the north and then north-east is rocky at first, with good views across the Wrynose Pass on to the Crinkles and Bowfell but the rocks soon give way to grass, and the continuation of the ridge is perfectly obvious down Wet Side Edge, pointing directly at Little Langdale Tarn. About half way down the ridge you will reach a large cairn, on a subsidiary hump of rock and grass, and this is a good spot from which to take a backward glance at the route, at the unusual steepness of the ground falling from Great Carrs, at the profile of the Prison Band. I sat here on one occasion watching in some surprise as about a dozen people, who did not look like fellwalkers, toiled on foot up the tarmac of the Wrynose Pass far below. Then, with a great roaring of its engine, a

minibus chugged past them and just made it to the top of the pass, where it waited for them. It was clear enough that its clutch was knackered and I hoped that it was not going to attempt to cross Hardknott Pass as well.

Beyond here, as the angle eases even more, another cairn marks where a path veers off to the left, heading for the top of the Wrynose Pass. It is much used, a testimony to the desire of even hardy fellwalkers to park their cars at the highest possible point of a convenient road. Our path down the rest of the ridge becomes much less obvious from here onwards as it turns and twists down a series of rock humps, trending to the right on the descent and allowing a good view of Greenburn's old copper works and dam. The old miners' paths can now also be clearly traced going up Birk Fell. There is no specific point at which to leave the ridge: simply work down the steep grass slope to re-cross the beck, the River Brathay, outside the intake wall, then back up the short slope to the car. It ends a memorable round.

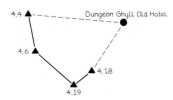

5 THE OXENDALE HORSESHOE

BEST MAP: *OS 1:25 000 Outdoor Leisure 6, South Western area*
APPROXIMATE TIME: *6½ hours*
TERRAIN: *Mostly on clearly defined paths which are mainly over rough and stony ground. There is one awkward step (avoidable) on Crinkle Crags.*

ITINERARY	Book & Fell No	Height of ascent	Distance of ascent	Cumulative distance	Height above sea level	
		feet	miles	miles	feet	mtrs
DUNGEON GHYLL OLD HOTEL					350	107
Pike o' Blisco	4.18	2100	2.25	2.25	2304	705
Cold Pike	4.19	650	1.25	3.50	2259	701
Crinkle Crags	4.06	850	1.50	5.00	2816	859
Bowfell	4.04	850	1.50	6.50	2960	902
DUNGEON GHYLL OLD HOTEL			3.00	9.50	350	107
Totals of heights and distances of ascent		4450	9.50			

AW's opinion was that Crinkle Crags gives 'Lakeland's best ridge-mile' and he was surely right. This splendid circuit, however, also includes Pike o' Blisco, Cold Pike (which, AW also pointed out, has three crinkles of its own) and Bowfell. When it is added that Oxendale has some of the finest ravines in the Lake District, the prospect of this round is mouthwatering.

The best start is the Dungeon Ghyll Old Hotel at the head of Great Langdale, but the National Trust car park there is understandably popular and it will pay to get there early. (Alternative parking may be found just over half a mile eastwards down the valley by the New Hotel.) The first top of the day is the shapely pyramid of Pike o' Blisco, so turn along the minor road towards Blea Tarn and Little Langdale, passing Wall End Farm, and then steeply uphill, where the road is unfenced. Just beyond the first sharp

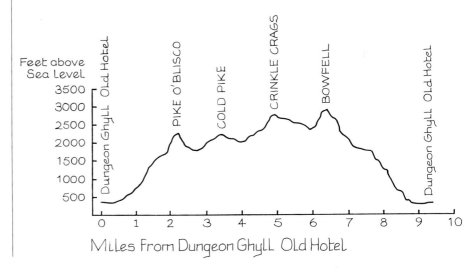

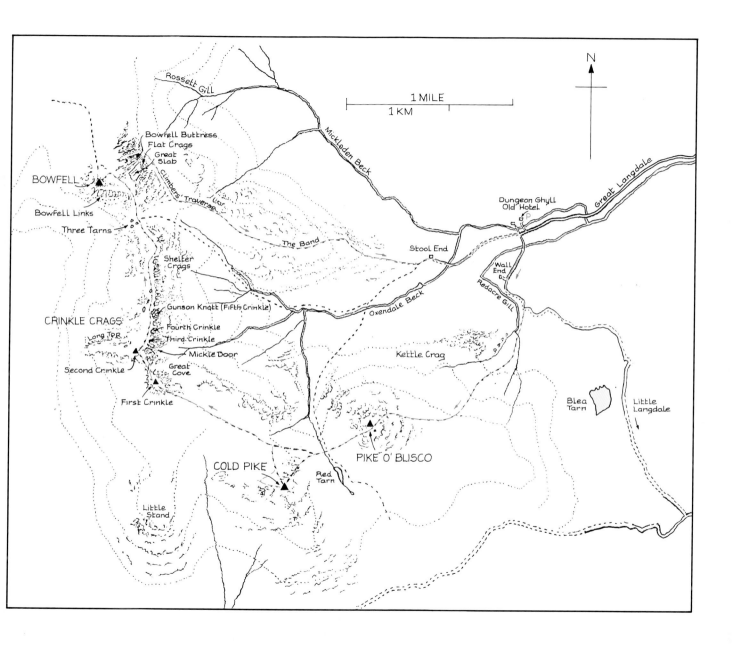

N

Rossett Gill

Mickleden Beck

1 MILE
1 KM

Great Langdale

Bowfell Buttress
Flat Crags
Great Slab

Dungeon Ghyll
Old Hotel

BOWFELL

Climbers' Traverse

Bowfell Links

Three Tarns

The Band

Stool End

Wall End

Shelter Crags

Redacre Gill

Oxendale Beck

Gunson Knott (Fifth Crinkle)

CRINKLE CRAGS

Fourth Crinkle

Third Crinkle

Long Top

Kettle Crag

Mickle Door

Second Crinkle

Great Cove

Blea Tarn

Little Langdale

First Crinkle

COLD PIKE

Red Tarn

PIKE O' BLISCO

Little Stand

bend a path turns off to the right towards Redacre Gill, on its left bank. After 300 paces the gill forks, the right-hand branch being a deeply cut and tree-filled ravine on the left side of the rocky Kettle Crag. The main gill is the left branch and the path crosses the stream at a jumble of boulders to climb the tongue of land between them. The path is fearfully stony and loose, in places a river of stones about six feet wide and would benefit from the 'pitching' that has been so excellently carried out, mostly by the National Trust, on some other similar paths.

Once over the lip at the head of the gill, however, the angle eases and the path slants towards Pike o' Blisco, which is now clearly in view ahead, buttressed by tilted, flat-topped rocks, one of which, to the left of the path, is particularly large and noticeable. Cairns now mark the way over slabs and occasional peaty ground to reach a weakness, a shallow gully, in the first of several bands of broken rocks. This gives a very easy scramble of about 15ft. A little higher, a second similar gully weakness is used for another little 10-ft scramble, while higher still is a third, maybe 20ft high but also easy-angled. Experts will hardly notice any of them. The path then arrives at the summit area between the two tops, each sporting a cairn, although that on the right, perched on an upthrust of grey rocks delightfully tinged with pink, is clearly the higher point. The cairn, although good and solid, is not a complete replacement for the tall column that AW knew and illustrated. The other cairn, the south one, is built on flat slabs.

Cold Pike is well seen from here, to the south-west across the depression containing Red Tarn, and a good although rough path leads down south-west from the top of Pike o' Blisco to the hause just north of Red Tarn. Here it links with the well-used track rising from Oxendale via Stool End that trends below Cold Pike on its way to Crinkle Crags, thus omitting Cold Pike. But Cold Pike doesn't deserve the cold shoulder. It can be easily reached with just a little more time and effort. An ill-defined ridge of rockier ground with a few boulders curves up to Cold Pike from the far (western) side of the hause, so that if you follow the main track for just a short distance and then turn off it to the left, this ridge can be used to reach its knobbly top. There are three distinct summits, all of the same lovely grey-pink rock that is found on Pike o' Blisco. It also has at least four cairns, two of them on the highest ground. The summit cairn is without doubt built on a solid rock platform with a square spike of naked rock protruding from it. This cairn overlooks Oxendale while fifty paces away is another cairn with a view towards Wrynose, Harter Fell and the attractively rocky fell of Little Stand. This does not rank as a 'Wainwright top', but I would rate it as infinitely better than the tedious top of Sour Howes, which is even more boring than Mungrisdale Common, both of which do!

Cold Pike is clearly an extension of the Crinkle Crags ridge but before continuing along it an interesting diversion can be made to seek what AW called Cold Pike Tooth. Peter Linney, who was with me on this walk, and I went searching for it, after a bit seriously wondering if the Lake District Vandal Society hadn't been at work – as recent newspaper reports suggest that they have been, on Ill Bell and at the head of Scandale. Eventually we did locate it. The 'crag west of the summit' is about 300 yards west (further than we expected), and is a substantial mass of steep, smooth rock, also facing west. The tooth of rock is at its foot, leaning at about 50 degrees and it has two very obvious fangs. I gauged it about 8ft high.

The bee-line from Cold Pike towards Crinkle Crags involves not just a simple walk over grass but some splodging through bog as well, so it is as well now to head for the motorway path heading in the same direction because it stays on drier land. Once joined, it is found to be a broad highway of bleached white stones running out onto firm ground as height is gained. Approaching the First Crinkle the path swings left and climbs onto its rocks, but it is worth trending to the right before going up further for a splendid view across Great Cove to the Second (highest) and Third Crinkles which are separated by the deep scree ravine of Mickle Door. (Incidentally, AW numbered these according to the direction of travel, *see* Crinkle Crags 11 and 13.)

The First Crinkle is the longest, about 300 yards long, and is quite crinkly itself, having several rocky humps. From the cairn on the highest of these there is a good view, the first of many to come, across Upper Eskdale to Cam Spout Crag, Scafell and Scafell Pike. An obvious broad depression is then reached before the rise up to the Second Crinkle, the rocky slope of which is split by a gully blocked by two flat-topped chock-stones, one on top of the other. This is the so-called 'bad step' of the Crinkles and a few timid souls may feel that its appearance is so frightening as to cause them to traverse out to the left before reaching the gully and thus avoid it. I may add I have never seen any-body do this and the actual ascent is very straightforward. It is, in fact, possible (although fairly inelegant for middle-aged ladies or gentlemen) to squeeze below the chock-stones and up the dirty chute behind it, but this is much better in winter when snow and ice make it quite a pleasant clamber. The normal way up is about 10ft of easy, although now polished, rock on the right, leading immediately to an easy rubble-covered ramp. This soon leads to what is clearly the highest point of the ridge before reaching Bowfell, seen ahead to the north. It is worth noting that this Second Crinkle projects a long ridge to the west, towards Eskdale; this is called Long Top and there is a path, and a few cairns, along its crest. This can be misleading in mist, especially to walkers coming in the opposite direction. The general direction of the ridge is south–north (and it is about one mile from the start of the Crinkles to the depression of Three Tarns) and this is well worth remembering in mist, for the path along the top drifts from the Oxendale side to the Eskdale side and back again and thus the immediate compass bearing varies.

From the Second Crinkle a short descent to the *north-east* reaches the head of Mickle Door with its steep-sided rock walls, bed of scree, and view to Pike o' Blisco. The most used path now by-passes the tops of the Third and Fourth Crinkles (which are fairly close together) on their left (east) sides, although they can both be visited easily. It then rises

Peter Linney in action on the awkward step on the Second Crinkle.

The Great Slab on Bowfell.

up and curves around the left shoulder of the Fifth, called Gunson Knott, followed by a fairly steep descent over rough rocks to a col, where there is a little tarn just below the path on the left. (This col gives an easy escape to Oxendale down scree and then grass.) The path now rises again, moving out briefly onto the right (Oxendale) side of the ridge, but then immediately swings back left and passes another tiny tarn. The traverse along the top of Shelter Crags now follows (whose extent and steepness may be appreciated when seen from The Band on the final descent) and the path then slants across a rocky and grassy slope towards a large tower-like mass of rock. It passes this on the left and runs out onto the depression of Three Tarns, where several outcrops hide the tarns themselves until you are almost upon them. A few smaller puddles help to further confuse the identity of the area but there is no mistaking the six or seven rock buttresses of Bowfell Links now rearing up ahead.

Almost immediately the path leading ahead (north-west, ignore one going left here) passes very close to the top edge of the extraordinary Great Slab, which is on the right. This vast sheet of rock is like a giant billiard table, tilted, but only slightly so that the stones and rocks littering its surface do not roll off. With care, it is possible to walk about upon it. At its lower edge, loose stones and boulders have collected to form a sloping scree corridor and a cairn marks where a path goes down this. Take note of this cairn and the path, for it marks where the descent begins.

The splendid summit of Bowfell must first be visited, however, so continue on the well-marked and cairned path to the north-west, climbing over small rocks onto bigger ones and finally, swinging in an arc to the left, over large boulders to the fine rock cone on the very top. So splendid is the panorama from here that you will be lucky to have the summit to yourself. The Crinkles are now put into perspective (looking north to south and with the advantage of height) as a broad rocky ridge rising gradually from the depression of Three Tarns (and you can at last actually see three tarns) to the Second (highest) Crinkle. There is a splendid view across Eskdale, down Great Langdale, in every direction. No wonder walkers linger here.

For the descent, return to the top of the Great Slab but, instead of stumbling back down the final ascent gully beside Bowfell Links, turn down the path, described above, which leads below the bottom edge of the Great Slab. This may well look as if it is heading into trouble but the path is a good one and the angle easy. On the way down there are grand views to Bowfell Buttress and to the head of Rossett Gill. At the bottom of Cambridge Crag, on the left of the path, there is a cool spring of water that I have never known to fail. As you reach the spring you also step onto a superb path called the Climbers' Traverse. This was originally developed by climbers contouring this north-east face of Bowfell to reach Bowfell Buttress, but it can obviously be used in the return direction (south-east) to reach the final descent ridge from Bowfell, called The Band.

The Climbers' Traverse is a delight, crossing some scree to another spring of sweet

The top of The Band, seen from the end of the Climbers' Traverse.

water at the base of Flat Crags, then keeping close to the foot of the steep rocks beyond, undulating along a narrow traverse, with steep ground falling away to Mickleden on the left. One of my dogs once slipped off this traverse one winter when the slope was so completely iced up that I was having to kick footholds. I watched in horror as he slithered downhill towards Mickleden, but he dug claws, his built-in crampons, into the snow and cautiously crept his way back to join me. He was more careful after that.

This splendid pathway ends all too soon, running out onto a stony shoulder descending to join the well-worn path down The Band. It is a pity that this shows so much erosion in places, but there is no denying its wonderful situation and consequent popularity, with superb views across Oxendale to Pike o' Blisco and to the Crinkles, and across Mickleden to the eye-catching Langdale Pikes. Near its foot, the path trends right to avoid short rock bluffs and then goes through a gate into the farmyard at Stool End, turning right and then along the tarmac farm track back to the road near the Old Dungeon Ghyll Hotel. They still serve a good pint, but it's a popular place and you may have to wait for it – during which you can reflect on your marvellous day!

ITINERARY	Book & Fell No	Height of ascent	Distance of ascent	Cumulative distance	Height above sea level	
		feet	miles	miles	feet	mtrs
Wha House (for Boot)					300	91
Slight Side	4.17	2300	3.25	3.25	2499	762
Scafell	4.02	750	1.25	4.50	3162	964
Scafell Pike	4.01	900	1.25	5.75	3210	978
Great End	4.03	350	1.33	7.08	2984	910
Esk Pike	4.05	425	1.25	8.33	2903	885
Bowfell	4.04	400	1.00	9.33	2960	902
Crinkle Crags	4.06	600	1.50	10.83	2816	859
Wha House			6.00	16.83	300	91
Totals of heights and distances of ascent		5725	16.83			

6 THE ESKDALE SKYLINE

Best Map: *OS 1:25 000 Outdoor Leisure 6, South Western area*
Approximate Time: *10–11 hours*
Terrain: *Some boggy stretches on the approach, otherwise on mostly firm or rocky ground on the high ridges.*

This marvellous walk is a high-level traverse of the six highest tops in the southern fells, some of the most rugged and exciting landscape in the Lake District. By virtue of its length (which also means that the scale of my sketch map has to be smaller than most in this book) and the difficult ground, it will be seen by most normal walkers as a challenge, requiring both physical fitness, daylight and reasonable conditions. But what a day to remember!

The starting point is a footpath just 300 yards west of Whahouse Bridge and opposite Wha House Farm in glorious Eskdale. There are a few places to park a car on the verge near the stile (grid ref 201009), but otherwise the hospitable Woolpack Inn is just over half a mile west down the valley. The path is indistinct at first, where it climbs through

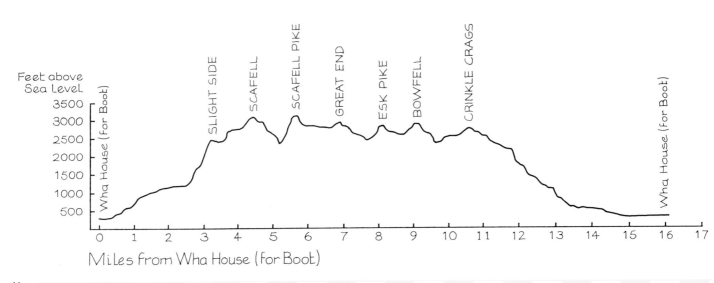

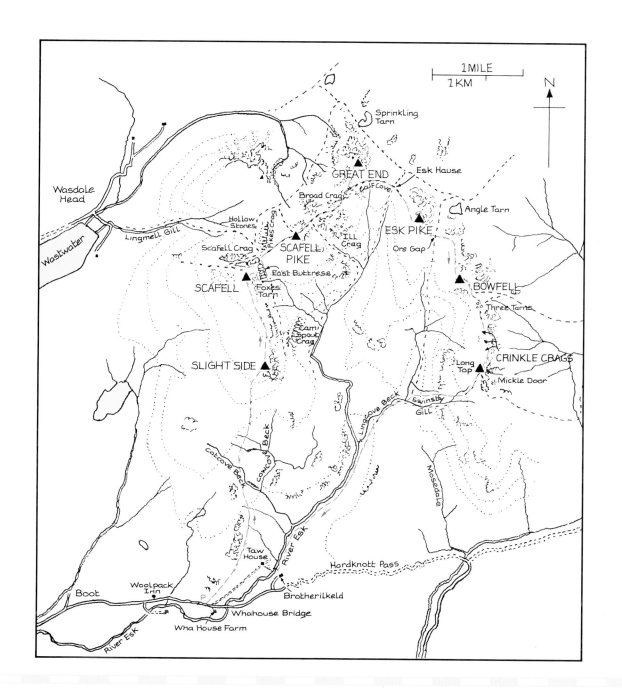

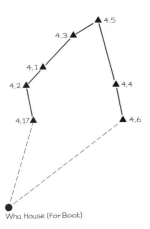

Wha House (for Boot)

boulders to the north-east, but you can be sure you have found it when it passes through a group of three sheep pens and then shadows the intake wall, traversing a series of slanting shelves below rock outcrops; these have caused this path to be known as the Terrace Route. As height is slowly gained there are pleasing views to enjoy across Eskdale and you will be able to pick out the remains of the Roman fort of Hardknott Castle. Cairns mark the way on this good but fairly rough path and the domed end of the fell of Slight Side will be seen rising ahead, beckoning, but still some way off. Reaching a boggy basin, the path goes round little outcrops and then joins Catcove Beck. The vista ahead now opens out and the path, which has been over rising land so far, leaves the stream and contours across the head of the big moss drained by Cowcove Beck, keeping at a lower altitude than might have been expected. You can't go on like this for ever as it is too easy; you have to gain height or you will never reach Slight Side.

When the turn uphill does come it is marked by a large flat boulder with a cairn on its top. It is the beginning of a steady uphill trudge that you knew had to come, that cannot be avoided and must therefore be endured. The path slants up a long grassy slope which steepens as height is gained. You scrabble up scree and claw a way between boulders, emerging onto a tilted grassy shelf. The path appears to end at a gap, a point where a boulder is trapped between large blocks of rock. This, at last, is Slight Side. The summit cairn is on top of the solid grey rocks on the left (upper) side of the gap and you will need to scramble to reach it. Such a fine little summit is some reward for the struggle on the last part of the ascent.

The path continues across a slight depression of grass and scattered stones then rises steadily for about half a mile along the edge of the escarpment, passing the point where a curving ridge leads down on the right towards Cam Spout Crag. More grass and stones, followed by a very rough and bouldery patch, and then, with mounting excitement, you are galloping along a flat rock crest to the windbreak and cairn on Scafell. It may prove a bit of a disappointment, for the cairn is built at the top of a very ordinary slope of rocks. But only about 200 yards away to the north is one of the grandest rock precipices in the Lake District, the north face of Scafell, and you are almost looking over it. A slight descent to a flat and grassy hause between outcrops (marked by a cairn and a key place on the mountain) and then a level stroll over rocky ground towards a large detached rock brings you to the head of Deep Gill. If you've never been here before you will almost certainly think 'What a marvellous view' and then, 'Oh ye gods! How on earth am I going to get down *there*?' *There* being a vertical drop of about 500ft where Deep Gill drops into dank and gloomy depths, and where dropped stones send back echoes making you realise that you are perched on the edge of an abyss. Scafell Pike is only about a mile away, as the crow flies. But you ain't no crow.

There are four routes from Scafell to Scafell Pike, three of which I will briefly mention because their existence is part of mountaineering and fellwalking history, and

Looking back along the Slight Side ridge to Eskdale, from near Scafell.

the fourth I recommend. They all begin from this flat grassy hause. First, if you head directly for Scafell Pike, to the north-east and beyond the grassy hause, you will naturally go towards the edge of the steep rocks and find an obvious path trending a little to the right and leading down a line of rocky grooves at an easy angle. If you are a competent rock-climber you will be able to descend the overhanging rock-corner that you will shortly reach and which quickly leads to the narrow arête of Mickledore, for this is the rock-climber's descent route. As a fellwalker without such experience, you are quite likely to fall off and hurt yourself, so don't bother coming down here.

Secondly, you will probably have heard of Lord's Rake. This used to be the usual way up or down, and if you turn down left (north-west) from the grassy hause, down a steepening stony slope, keeping right, you will spot the Lord's Rake path turning back sharp right to traverse in a slanting line across the face of the crags. The path dips down to a little col between the steep wall on the right and a short pinnacle on the left and then dips again before completing the final slanting descent down a trough, passing the entry to the West Wall Traverse of Deep Gill (see next route) and arriving at the bottom of the crags. AW says that: 'The Rake is unique, and one's fellwalking education is not complete until its peculiar delights and horrors have been experienced.' Unfortunately the increasing erosion over the last fifteen years in particular has made the horrors outweigh the delights. On the rare occasions when there is good snow into which you can kick steps it is still a good route, but most of the time the path is now slimy and wet and the risk of slipping and either causing or experiencing an accident is high.

The third way is the West Wall Traverse which starts from the top of Deep Gill (that abyss down which you peered a short time ago) and then joins Deep Gill and which I have ascended and descended many times in both winter and summer conditions. However, before writing this chapter, I went up and down it to check its current condition and have *no hesitation* in saying that this too has now become very worn and probably dangerous. As a descent especially I think it is now best avoided unless you are experienced in the peculiar delights of creeping down steep, disintegrating rock with a considerable drop below your feet. It is easier in ascent, but not much. I recommend you leave it alone.

The fourth alternative is the way that I would unhesitatingly recommend now to any fellwalker: the descent to Foxes Tarn. From the grassy hause, turn *right* (east) immediately and then a line of cairns leads down a splendid rock staircase, zigzagging down what used to be an awful slope of shifting scree. This new path was built by the National Trust and they deserve the thanks and support of all fellwalkers for so doing. The laid stones end at the tiny Foxes Tarn, from where you have a view to Scafell Pike, then the path descends rougher ground down a wide gully used by a little stream. At its foot you turn back left uphill for about 400ft, on a path up scree below the overhanging walls of Scafell's East Buttress, to reach Mickledore. The path now crosses this narrow arête, with views down to Hollow Stones on the left and to upper Eskdale on the right, then ascends gradually over very stony ground to the north-east. The path clambers over big boulders in places and although these have been well scratched by boots the cairns are still of real value in mist or snow. As befitting the highest point in England, the stony top of Scafell Pike is crowned with a huge cairn like the base of a slightly collapsing tower, and of course it overtops the trig point nearby. I counted no fewer than eight stone windbreaks nearby recently, but visitors here, who may vary in number from nil up to a hundred or more on a fine day, generally cluster round the cairn, and always in good, if often perspiring, humour. They've done it! *You* have a lot more still to do.

Lingmell (left) from near Calf Cove. In the background are Red Pike and Pillar.

Although the path from Scafell Pike to Esk Hause is the main 'motorway' route undulating along the ridge, there is no smooth tarmac for it is over the roughest ground in the Lakes. Fortunately there are cairns and the blazed scratches of earlier generations of nailed boots to make it difficult to lose the way. The descent is off to the north-east, over big flat stones then soon skittering down rubble and earth to the narrow hause, Broad Crag col, at the head of Little Narrowcove. (A path descends to upper Eskdale down the scree and earth slope on the right from the col and would be a good escape route if one were needed.) Then a rough ascent over rocks bypasses the top of Broad Crag; this is seldom visited because it is defended by a tumbled mass of jagged boulders, but it is a grand viewpoint to Wasdale. More rugged ground leads to a second col, this time by-passing the top of Ill Crag, another fine viewpoint over Eskdale to Bowfell, Crinkle Crags and much of the route still to come. An easier plateau then leads to perhaps the roughest ground of all traversed by the path, where youngsters may skip along but old codgers place their feet carefully as they teeter along a rock pavement of tilted blocks. This ends suddenly on much easier ground where the main path trends right and descends to grass and a little stream in Calf Cove. This is where Victorian tourists used to leave their ponies before completing the ascent to Scafell Pike on foot.

Just before the drop down to Calf Cove a further path leads forward, rising slightly, just east of north, and follows a grassy strip across the plateau between rougher and stonier ground on either side. This leads to the main summit cairn of Great End, built on bigger rocks and with a windbreak constructed directly below it. There is no view from here worthy of this grand mountain but you will see that there is another large cairn, to the north-west. A curving walk towards it, arcing well to the right as you go, will enable you to peer down Central Gully and enjoy tremendous views over Sprinkling Tarn to Borrowdale and Skiddaw and even to the Langdale Pikes.

Return from the *summit* cairn to the SSW along the grassy strip (the apparently direct line is over a mass of rough boulders and is very unpleasant) to Calf Cove and now join the main path descending to Esk Hause. Paths descend from this open and windswept col: to the south to upper Eskdale and to the north-east to another major hause where there is a four-sided windbreak, but the path you need is an *ascending* one to the south-east. It is well cairned and frequently passes over rock ledges just tilted enough in your favour as you climb, leading to a little gully and a direct approach up the rocks onto Esk Pike's summit. In fact, the path swings left and dodges the actual top by a few yards.

Heading for Esk Pike one day with my pal Roger and my two dogs, we passed three walkers going the other way. Freddie is my older dog and gets a bit tired on a long day so, when one of the walkers said quietly in German what sounded like *'Der lezte ist fertig'*, which I translated mentally as 'The last one is knackered', I thought the remark was about Freddie. I then realised that it was Roger who was fifty yards behind at the time. I must add that it was not true. He was, like me, just half-knackered.

Bowfell is the next top. A steady, although rocky descent on an obvious path leads in about fifteen minutes to the Ore Gap, where hematite ore makes the earth look noticeably red. Then a rising line of cairns curves towards Bowfell, mostly over rock although you do reach a little grassy col from where you can peer over and down to Mickleden beyond the head of Bowfell Buttress. A last short walk across a boulder field and an easy scramble up the final rock pyramid leads to the top of yet another marvellous mountain. It's a wonderful place to be, with a glorious view in every direction.

A long way below to the south-east you will see the Three Tarns glinting on their depression and, beyond them, a rising ridge of crumpled rocky land climbs to your final top of the day, the highest of the Crinkle Crags (which is the fourth when going in this direction; AW numbered them chronologically according to the direction of travel – *see* Crinkle Crags 11 and 13). Descend the rocks and pick up the cairned path leading roughly east towards the Great Slab, which is well seen on this descent, tilted towards the head of Mickleden. This path passes beyond the Slab and then turns steeply south down an eroded gully, a route taken to avoid the buttresses and gullies of Bowfell Links, which are not really seen until you are beyond them.

The walk along the ridge of the Crinkle Crags which now follows is full of interest, the path winding up and down, twisting and turning from the Eskdale side of the ridge to the Oxendale side and back again. But there are also variations on the path and it can be very confusing in poor conditions, when it is important to watch for certain land-marks. (The map for Walk 5, The Oxendale Horseshoe, on page 39, may be helpful as it shows the Crinkle Crags area in more detail.) Passing through the little maze of outcrops partly hiding the Three Tarns, the ridge route goes by a large tower-like mass of rock on its right side and then slants up grooves bearing left and along the rough top of Shelter Crags. Pass one tiny tarn and shortly after it notice a second tarn, just below the path and to its right, on a grassy depression. Immediately beyond this the ridge path rises sharply up a jumble of large rocks and round the shoulder of Gunson Knott, the Fifth Crinkle. The path then curves round the shoulders of the next two Crinkles to reach another hause, a key depression, from where the scree shoot of Mickle Door drops sharply between rock walls towards Oxendale, on the left. I emphasise this because the rise beyond is up onto the Second Crinkle, from where the descent begins to Eskdale again. In good conditions there will be no doubt when you are on the Second Crinkle as it is the highest point on the ridge. It throws a long subsidiary spur, Long Top, towards Eskdale, which could possibly give a descent route but it ends in a rash of outcrops and steep crags that are much better suited to ascent than descent.

The best way is to leave the summit down a cairned path which is initially to the WSW but quickly starts to curve back left and starts contouring. You will realise that this is a footpath linking the First and Second Crinkles, avoiding the awkward little gully (the direct route) on the latter. At its lowest point, you must just leave this path and turn off downhill, on pathless grass, following the course of a stream flowing towards Swinsty Gill. When the slope shortly steepens noticeably, your toes start banging against the end of your boots and the stream heads for a rocky-sided ravine, it is easier to leave it and just go straight down. A conveniently easy and dry gully leads lower still to easier-angled and still-grassy slopes, and you will soon join the footpath beside Lingcove Beck.

There are a few slutchy bits of ground to cross and then a fairly rough descent, with the stream tumbling down attractive cascades on the right. The path becomes a good hard surface as it reaches two sheepfolds and a little packhorse bridge, Lingcove Bridge, at the point where Lingcove Beck joins the River Esk. Here there are some marvellous pools for swimming, a temptation that I have often failed to resist, and then the route continues on a lovely path down Eskdale. It stays lovely until it avoids a boggy patch of ground by rising away from the river and through a rash of boulders, an unwelcome change for tired legs that thought they were going downhill all the way. Happily the uphill bit is short and, beyond a stile, you are soon able to ramble through fields, avoiding the sheep maternity wards by using the specially fenced path beside the river. For the final stretch, cross the footbridge and follow the path beyond that leads to Taw House, then turn left along the farm track. You may get a lovely whiff of woodsmoke as you pass the little cottage nearing the road and rejoin your car. Like Roger, Freddie and me, you will probably be completely knackered, but it will have been worth it.

Looking back from near Esk Pike to the Gables and Great End.

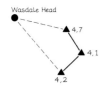

Wasdale Head

4,7

4,1

4,2

7 THE LINGMELL CIRCUIT

BEST MAP: *OS 1:25 000 Outdoor Leisure 6, South Western area*
APPROXIMATE TIME: *5½ hours*
TERRAIN: *A real mixture of firm paths, grass, and some very rough although generally well-marked ground.*

ITINERARY	Book & Fell No	Height of ascent	Distance of ascent	Cumulative distance	Height above sea level	
		feet	miles	miles	feet	mtrs
WASDALE HEAD					250	76
Lingmell	4.07	2450	2.50	2.50	2649	807
Scafell Pike	4.01	850	0.88	3.38	3210	978
Scafell	4.02	850	1.25	4.63	3162	964
WASDALE HEAD			3.75	8.38	250	76
Totals of heights and distances of ascent		4150	8.38			

To walk this splendid circuit is not merely to exercise the body but to store wonderful memories of walled green fields lapped by Wastwater, the Lake District's deepest tarn, and of the soaring grey crags of England's highest mountain, which will be seen at close hand.

The true ridge route to Lingmell, with which this round begins, starts up what AW calls The Shoulder, and it can be gained from either the parking place on the approach to the Wasdale Head Inn or, slightly more easily, from the National Trust camp-site at the head of Wastwater, where cars may also be parked off the track (grid ref 183075). From the site, a path leads up beside Lingmell Gill, shortly reaching a kissing-gate and a notice advising about the new path to Hollow Stones built by the National Trust and

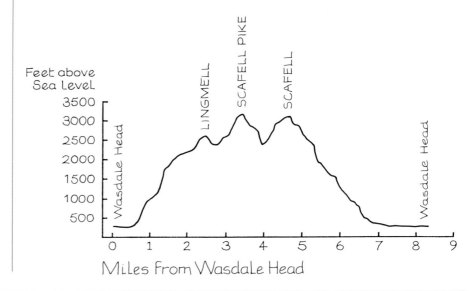

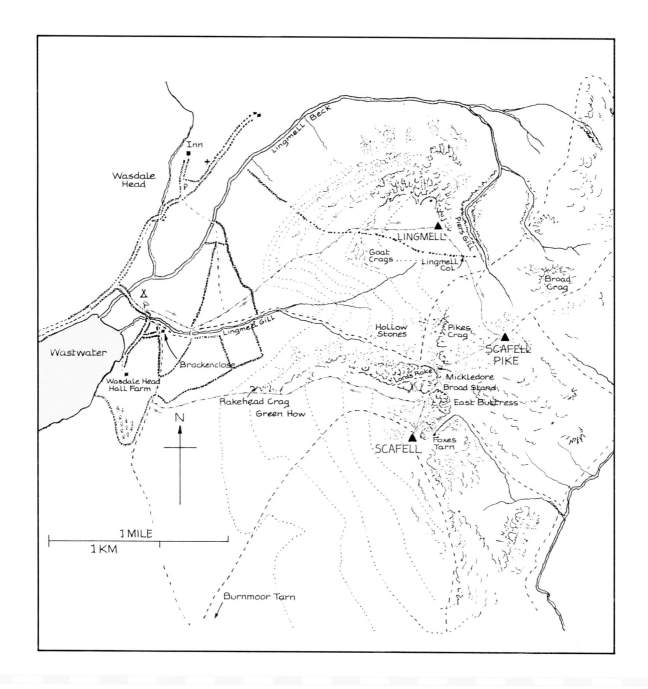

Wasdale
Head

Inn

P

Wastwater

Brackenclose

Wasdale Head
Hall Farm

Rakehead Crag
Green How

N

1 MILE

1 KM

Lingmell Beck

Lingmell Gill

LINGMELL

Goat
Crags

Lingmell
Col

Piers Gill

Broad
Crag

Hollow
Stones

Pikes
Crag

SCAFELL
PIKE

Lords Rake

Mickledore
Broad Stand

East Buttress

SCAFELL

Foxes
Tarn

Burnmoor Tarn

The Lingmell Gill skyline seen from Wastwater.

opened in April 1994. Immediately beyond this kissing-gate and before you have had any chance to check out the new path, turn left and then immediately right, on a much fainter path heading up the long spur thrown down by Lingmell to the south-west towards Wastwater. It gives a steady ascent on grass and through bracken, a slope on which a few isolated hawthorns flourish, firstly crossing the path rising from Wasdale Head and then a transverse wall by a ladder-stile. At a little over a thousand feet above the start, the grass turns to rock and scree but soon reverts to grass and bilberry; the spur now comes to an end and the path runs out onto a broad plateau where there is a cairn.

A fairly long but easy-angled ascent over grass and bilberry now stretches ahead until grey rocks appear, the outliers of Goat Crags, consolidating into substantial outcrops which look, from a distance, like the summit rocks. The view from here to Hollow Stones, Pikes Crag and the great north-face cliffs of Scafell is truly excellent. There is, however, still a little depression to cross, traversed by a collapsing wall which totters as far as Lingmell Col and, beyond the wall, as you continue still heading east, can be seen an elegant, pyramid-shaped cairn on what is probably the highest group of rocks, although a rival group about forty yards to the north could put up a good case to be the summit.

What is not in dispute is that the cairn, when reached, is on a superb rocky view-point on the edge of a terrific drop, with the giant ravine of Piers Gill directly below. Great Gable is an equally splendid sight from here, but will be appreciated even more if you walk about 300 yards to the north, descending slightly over rocky but easily crossed ground. Here, on an even better viewpoint than the summit, is another tall and slender cairn, almost a needle, overlooking the head of Wasdale. Don't fail to find time to visit this one. I don't think it was here in AW's day.

Returning to the summit, then keeping the steep ground on the left hand, go down the slope to Lingmell Col, crossed by the remnants of the wall, and up the slope beyond. Now either join the cairned path coming up from Hollow Stones or another further left which is also cairned but much nearer to the edge of the amphitheatre below Broad Crag. These shortly join and the path then winds uphill, with cairns almost every five yards. It looks very obvious and impossible to lose the way but once, in mist and in descent, after climbing an ice gully on Great End, I did go wrong somewhere here, ended up in Wasdale instead of in Borrowdale and had to get a taxi back all the way round the coast. Ten quid was a fortune in those days. Just to be sure, the final compass direction across the stony wilderness is south-east, and brings you to the huge flat-topped circular cairn (the summit trig is nearby) on the summit of Scafell Pike. On the north side a plaque commemorates the men of the Lakes who fell in the 1914–18 war and also the fact that the summit was given to the nation, under the custody of the National Trust, by Charles Henry Baron Leconfield in 1919. You might have to climb over a few resting bodies to be able to reach and read it.

The short distance between Scafell Pike and the next top, Scafell, is the most compli-cated mile or so of land in the Lake District. The cairned route leaving the top of Scafell Pike heads to the north for a few yards down the jumble of rocks but then swings left (west). Keep going west, ignoring a branch off to the right, and head directly for the great cliffs of Scafell facing you. It is a very stony descent, often over jagged boulders, to reach the narrow ridge of Mickledore, where there is a bit of grass and a mountain rescue box containing a stretcher and other equipment.

Just left of the point where Mickledore abuts against the cliff wall, a slanting gully and sloping rocks are an obvious line of weakness by which to gain the top of the cliffs above, but this is Broad Stand, the rock-climbers' descent route, and it has an awkward overhanging wall blocking the way at a crucial and unavoidable point. So give up thoughts of tackling it – unless, of course, you are a rock-climber or wish to test the efficiency of the stretcher. The old traditional way to go is via Lord's Rake, gained by descending shaly ground at the foot of the crags on the right-hand side of Mickledore and then following a slanting line of weakness across the crags, passing the foot of Deep Gill (which allows entry to a variation known as the West Wall Traverse into Deep Gill). But Lord's Rake has suffered a great deal of wear and tear over recent years, and except under rarely encountered conditions of firm snow, it is now usually wet and slippery with a consequent high risk of either causing an accident or being involved in one. The lower part of Lord's Rake has to be climbed before entry can be gained to the West Wall Traverse into Deep Gill, but the upper part of Deep Gill, beyond the Traverse, is now equally worn and dangerous. Experts will recognise the conditions and be able to cope with them, but all other fellwalkers are strongly advised not to attempt Lord's Rake or the West Wall Traverse.

I can really only recommend one route by which to gain Scafell from Mickledore and that is via Foxes Tarn, a route which has been made far better than it ever was by the excellent work of the National Trust in the last year or so. For this, descend left from Mickledore beneath the overhanging crags of the East Buttress and a path will be found leading down about 400ft to a point below the left end of the cliffs at the foot of a square-cut stony and steep gully, which has a stream coming down it. There is a cairn at its foot. Now, up we go. It is rough but easy scrambling to the top of the square-cut part of the gully, then up easier ground beyond to reach the tiny Foxes Tarn, little more than a puddle with a large rock in it, but allowing a good view back to Scafell Pike. Above Foxes Tarn is what used to be a dreadful scrabble up loose scree but is now a stone staircase, clearly built with enormous effort and expense. It is a splendid way up, thanks to the National Trust, but no thanks to those motorists who are too mean to pay a quid or so to use the NT car parks and so block up the roads in Great Langdale and elsewhere. This fine path ends at a large cairn, with another about 8ft away from it forming a sort of gateway; then a line of cairns continues south-west to the summit. This can be visited shortly but, before doing so, you must have a look at the real views.

Twenty yards beyond the point where the path emerges onto the summit plateau is a grassy hause between stony outcrops. Turning right (north) from here for about 80 yards, towards an obvious isolated rock, brings you to the top of the chasm of Deep Gill. You can look across it for a fine view to Great Gable and Kirk Fell, and down it – and you will appreciate why it is no longer an attractive ascent or descent route.

The cairned path from the grassy hause leads you quickly to the cairn and windbreak on Scafell's top. It is a more comfortable place to sit for a while, but the views to the south, while long-ranging, lack the drama of those you have just been admiring. You

Great Gable seen from Scafell Pike over Broad Crag.

can, however, see Wastwater and Burnmoor Tarn and it is down these open western slopes that the descent to the valley begins.

Return to the grassy hause and turn left down a stony slope heading west, keeping the edge of the cliffs on your right hand. You will pass the point where the top of the Lord's Rake path emerges but continue beyond it on a reasonable, if fairly steep, path which keeps near the edge of the drop on the right into the combe of Hollow Stones. After 1500ft of descent you skirt the edge of Rakehead Crag (merely a few rocks on the edge of a shallow gill) where the path is very clear – but then it vanishes. It would appear that this, the Green How route, 'is as much out of fashion as the Victorians who favoured it', as AW says. But Victoriana is coming back into fashion and AW agreed that 'as a quick way down it is first-class'. You will soon pick up the path again, heading towards Wasdale Head Hall Farm and follow traces along the top of the intake wall to where it joins the Burnmoor Tarn track at a gate. Turn right here and the track leads alongside the wall, into the grounds of Brackenclose, the private hut owned by the Fell and Rock Climbing Club, out at the far side and back beside the Lingmell Beck to the camp-site.

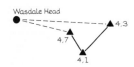

8 GREAT END AND THE SCAFELL PIKE CREST

BEST MAP: *OS 1:25 000 Outdoor Leisure 6, South Western area*
APPROXIMATE TIME: *5½ hours*
TERRAIN: *A mixture of all types, with paths over grass, scree and very rough, rocky ground. There is some easy scrambling on Great End.*

ITINERARY	Book & Fell No	Height of ascent	Distance of ascent	Cumulative distance	Height above sea level	
		feet	miles	miles	feet	mtrs
WASDALE HEAD					250	76
Great End	4.03	2800	3.25	3.25	2984	910
Scafell Pike	4.01	600	1.33	4.58	3210	978
Lingmell	4.07	280	0.88	5.46	2649	807
WASDALE HEAD			2.50	7.96	250	76
Totals of heights and distances of ascent		3680	7.96			

The ascent of Great End by the way of the steep ridge of The Band (not to be confused with the much better known Band on Bowfell) is the highlight of this circuit, giving a real sense of achievement. The continuation to Scafell Pike, England's highest mountain, and the descent down Lingmell are just thrown in for good measure! As AW rightly wrote: 'This is the true Lakeland of the fellwalker, the sort of terrain that calls him back time after time.'

Just before reaching the Wasdale Head Inn, where the road ends, it runs into an enclosed triangle of land where forty or more cars can park (grid ref 187085) and this is the best place from which to begin. From here a walled lane leads north-east, shortly passing the tiny St Olaf's church surrounded by yews. The path continues on the level

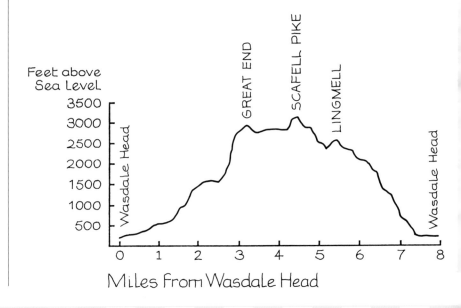

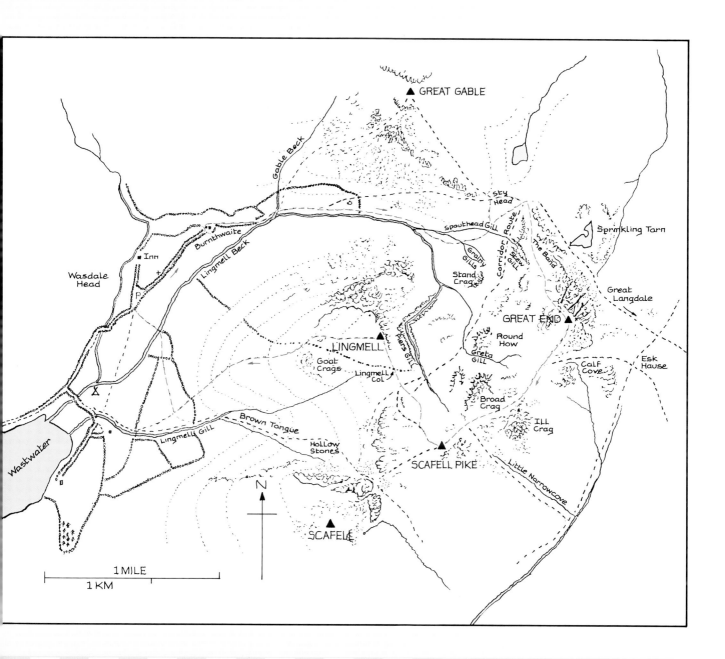

GREAT GABLE

Gable Beck

Sty Head

Spouthead Gill

Sprinkling Tarn

Burnthwaite

Inn

Grainy Gills

Corridor Route

Skew Gill

The Band

Lingmell Beck

Stand Crag

Great Langdale

Wasdale Head

GREAT END

Round How

Greta Gill

Piers Gill

Calf Cove

Esk Hause

LINGMELL

Goat Crags

Lingmell Col

Broad Crag

ILL Crag

Wastwater

Brown Tangue

Lingmell Gill

Hollow Stones

SCAFELL PIKE

Little Narrowcove

N

SCAFELL

1 MILE

1 KM

between walled fields, into the farm yard at Burnthwaite and out again immediately on the left. The sycamores by the farm and a final stand of larch trees are soon passed as the walls fan out, and the path crosses Gable Beck by a footbridge. In another hundred yards, beside the Lingmell Beck and below the crags of Lingmell itself high on the right, the broad path turns uphill and slants to where it cuts through a wall traversing the lower part of the fellside below Great Gable. Rather than just trudging along this motorway, which is fast but very boring, continue along it until just before reaching a collapsing sheepfold, then turn off to the right, keeping on the level. This is the old route to Sty Head. It is less direct, a little longer, and much more interesting. It is also still very little used, despite AW's advocacy of it nearly forty years ago. I may add that in the course of working on this and the preceding volume, I have found a number of instances where AW pointed out excellent routes, much superior to the usual obvious tourist ways, but where there is still little sign of foot-traffic. Such evidence does not give much support to the contention (that I have heard levelled at him) that AW is 'responsible' for the erosion of many popular paths in the Lake District.

The west face of Great End now dominates the view directly ahead to the south-east, and, looking from here, it is worth studying the scene. The deep-cut ravine is Greta Gill which, at its foot, joins the as yet unseen Piers Gill. Left of Greta Gill is Stand Crag and left again are the two much less incut channels of Grainy Gills. Further left still is the deep slanting gash of Skew Gill and behind that is the ridge of The Band, stretching up to Great End. From this angle in the valley The Band shows a fiercely steep face of rock falling towards Wasdale, but its crest is tiered and at a much more amenable angle. It is this skyline which will shortly provide the ridge route to Great End.

At a point about 50 yards above the junction of the Lingmell Beck with the stream from Piers Gill the path crosses over to the other (south) bank and then rises up grassy tongues towards The Band, with white stones gleaming like bleached bones in the grass. It then crosses over the water again to the left side, just below the junction of the two Grainy Gills, then starts to rise quite steeply, although still in graceful curves, to the top of a brow. Here the water of Spouthead Gill (the continuation below Skew Gill) tumbles over a little escarpment in a small waterfall and the path crosses just above it to join a very short pitched section (stones laid together). The path now turns its back on Great End and climbs instead towards Great Gable, quickly joining the motorway route just before reaching Sty Head (where there is a mountain rescue box on the hause). Rather than doing this, however, you can cut a corner by following a fainter path to the north-east across the basin ahead, keeping well left of the stream from Skew Gill and joining the obvious path of the Corridor Route, turning left along it.

The path of the Corridor Route meets the path between Sty Head and Great Langdale at an acute angle, bisected by the grass and rock ridge of The Band, our route to Great End. So turn right (east) up the path towards Esk Hause and Great Langdale,

but only for about fifty yards, then turn right again (SSE) and onto the ridge. This is an obvious natural route (and I do not understand why it has not had more traffic) and you simply rise easily up grass between little ledges on the crest to reach a shoulder, where a path appears. This path continues winding up the ridge, marked by cairns, until at about 800ft above the toe of the ridge you reach another shoulder and a grassy hollow at the head of Skew Gill. Above this, the slope steepens and the route scrambles up a short but easy gully with good holds. (The holds weren't so good for my dogs and I had to pull them up by heaving on their leads, which is perhaps why they aren't so keen as they used

Sprinkling Tarn and Seathwaite Fell with views down Borrowdale as far as Skiddaw.

to be when younger. Henry is also a lot stouter, he's getting middle-aged spread, just like humans.) Easier ground, with cairns, follows, passing above the top of Cust's Gully, to reach a wilderness of large boulders where the path seems to disappear. Clamber upwards over these for a short distance until the path reappears and almost immediately you step onto the summit plateau of Great End, right next to a cairn and windbreak.

This is not the official summit cairn, but a substantial one, nonetheless, the north-west cairn; the main cairn is on another rocky rise about 200 yards to the south-east, beyond a very slight depression. On the way over to it, ensure you trend left to peer down the most impressive Great End cliffs, and down Central Gully to Borrowdale and Sprinkling Tarn in particular. Fabulous views to complement a splendid ascent. When I was in my twenties and we used to have real winters with lots of snow and ice, I learnt how to brake with an ice-axe by repeatedly leaping down the upper part of the Great Gully. It was a skill that saved my life only a few years ago, but that is another story.

Leaving the summit cairn, head SSW and along a level grassy strip between rougher bouldery ground on either hand and in about 500 yards you will intersect with the major route for Scafell Pike coming via Esk Hause just above the grassy hollow of Calf Cove. Turn right (south-west) and a well-scored path will lead over a stretch of very rough ground, a pavement of tilted, sharp-edged rocks where you will be stepping from one to the other and hoping fervently that you don't do the splits. This leads to an easier plateau, then a dip to a depression which AW calls Ill Crag col (the cairn on Ill Crag being situated roughly 300 yards south) and to the traverse of a shoulder of Broad Crag. This again is over very rough ground with many jagged boulders, and reaches another narrow col at the head of the scree slide of Little Narrowcove: AW calls this Broad Crag col. If you look down on the right (north-west) you will see Lingmell and where the Corridor Route crosses the head of Piers Gill.

A last pull, up a shaly and rubbly ridge leading onto large flat stones, leads to the huge summit cairn on Scafell Pike. It's a grand place, the top of the roof of England, especially if you are on your own. When it is crowded, as it often is, then you will appreciate that quiet ascent to the peaceful summit of Great End.

The final top of the day is Lingmell, to the north-west and, having left the rough blocks around the summit pyramid of the Pike, a line of cairns, many cairns, leads in that direction. The path, essentially the continuation of the Corridor Route to Scafell Pike, descends fairly rapidly for about 800ft and in clear weather you will then have no difficulty in seeing the place where you leave it and descend easy ground just a little further to reach Lingmell col. In mist it would probably be best to give up thoughts of going to Lingmell (normal views will be obscured anyway) and stay on any path trending left (south-west) because it will lead into the cirque of Hollow Stones from where you will easily pick up paths leading down Lingmell Gill to the valley.

Cross the collapsing wall on Lingmell col and a faint path, still north-west, quickly

Lingmell, shadowed left, seen from the head of Little Narrowcove with Red Pike and Pillar seen just above the cloud inversion.

leads up the slope beyond, with the steep ground falling away on the right, to the tall pyramid of the cairn on Lingmell's summit. It is perched on a magnificent viewpoint, overlooking the tremendous ravine of Piers Gill, the biggest in the Lakes, with more dramatic views to Great Gable. As a viewpoint it rivals Great End and, if you have time, a short descent and a walk of about 300 yards to the north will take you to an even more elegant and slender cairn situated overlooking all the fells at the head of Wasdale.

The ridge descends initially to the west, on a faint path down rocky ground, continuing in that direction until the collapsing wall is crossed again and Goat Crags have been outflanked, then turns to the south-west down a long broad plateau of grass and bilberry. An isolated cairn marks where the plateau ends and the ridge turns more sharply downhill, with Wastwater now dominating the view below. Then, apart from a brief stretch where the path skitters down scree and rubble, the route continues down the grassy crest of the ridge. A ladder-stile is useful to cross a transverse wall, then just a little lower down you reach the path traversing across the toe of the ridge. Here you turn right, for Wasdale Head, and slant across a brackeny slope dotted with isolated hawthorns to a kissing-gate beneath a huge ash tree. In a further 250 yards a footbridge leads across the usually stony bed of a stream whose width bears witness to the power of the floods that can rush down it, then level meadows with ash trees and gorse lead to a gate and tarmac at a bend in the road. Turn right and in a hundred yards you'll be back at your car. I guarantee you will not quickly forget that splendid ascent route up The Band of Great End.

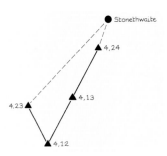

9 THE GLARAMARA RIDGE

BEST MAP: *Using a single map only, OS 1:50 000 Landranger 90 Penrith, Keswick & Ambleside area shows the whole walk but with barely enough detail. At 1:25 000 scale, both OS Outdoor Leisure 4, North Western area and 6, South Western area are needed and recommended in this case.*
APPROXIMATE TIME: *5½–6 hours*
TERRAIN: *The main part of the ridge has good paths on firm ground, but the approach and descent are over virtually untracked rocky or boggy ground.*

ITINERARY	Book & Fell No	Height of ascent	Distance of ascent	Cumulative distance	Height above sea level	
		feet	miles	miles	feet	mtrs
STONETHWAITE					315	96
Rosthwaite Fell	4.24	1500	1.50	1.50	1807	551
Glaramara	4.13	1000	1.75	3.25	2560	783
Allen Crags	4.12	500	1.75	5.00	2572	785
Seathwaite Fell	4.23	0	1.75	6.75	1970	601
STONETHWAITE			3.75	10.50	315	96
Totals of heights and distances of ascent		3000	10.50			

Rosthwaite Fell is an area of superbly wild and rocky land between Combe Gill and Langstrath. It is part of a broad and undulating ridge leading south-west on which there are three high points of land. Two of these are named, while one, which is also the highest, appears to be unnamed. The two named ones are separated by a depression containing the romantically named Tarn at Leaves and the lowest point, north of the tarn, is named Bessyboot. AW treated this as the summit of Rosthwaite Fell and I am therefore doing the same.

There is, however, another problem. The AW ridge-line map links Rosthwaite Fell to Glaramara and then to Allen Crags but unfortunately, and perhaps capriciously (especially since AW himself recognised that 'The Scafell *massif* has its roots in Borrow-

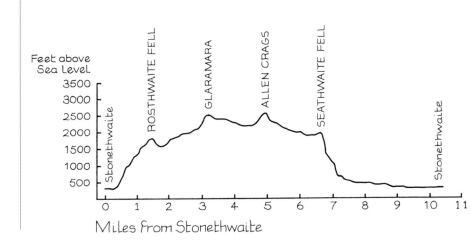

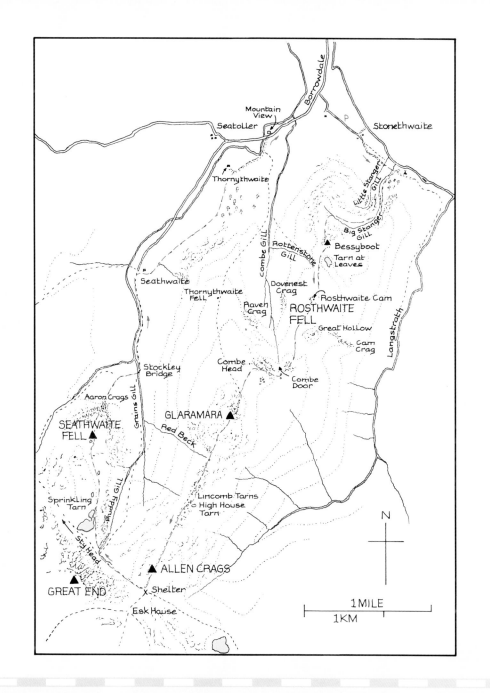

dale'), it ends there, on the doorstep of Scafell Pike and with your nose up against the north face of Great End. You have to get back to base somehow and although you could simply walk back on the good path down Ruddy Gill and Grains Gill, here is a grand opportunity to bag another appropriate Wainwright top, Seathwaite Fell, to give a good horseshoe round. The whole circuit is very fine and will appeal to those who like wild country, although it would be best avoided if there is any risk of misty conditions or poor visibility.

There is parking to be found on the wide verges of the minor road just before you enter the little village of Stonethwaite in Borrowdale (grid ref 262138). Then walk through it, passing the renovated Langstrath Hotel, and take the lane beyond (signed to the camp-site for vehicles) rather than the footpath. In about 300 yards, directly opposite the point where this lane turns left into the fields of the camp-site, there is a gate through the fence on the right. Here you are directly below two breaches in the rim of crags overlooking Stonethwaite, although they are hidden by trees. The major breach used by Big Stanger Gill is the route to the tops. Go through the gate and into the wood and climb steep fellside (it *feels* as if it is at least 45 degrees) beneath the oak trees. There is not much sign of a path to begin with, but as you trend rightwards a reasonable path materialises on the left edge of the stream. After about 350ft of ascent, you cross a small clearing and then continue up the left edge of a deep and very stony ravine to a good stone-slab stile over a wall (no longer the 'very awkward stile' that AW named). The path continues steeply through delightful landscape between crags on the left and the watercourse on the right, crossing the remnants of a collapsed wall and entering a little boggy amphitheatre on the lip of the ravine, about 900ft above the start. The amphitheatre is walled, but the wall has been down for years where it meets the stream and you can pass through the gap and cross the stream easily to its right bank. This bends right, with a little cascade, and although the dramatic part of the gill has now been left behind, the water flows in a shallow ravine for a little further before trending rightwards. Ignore a tempting grassy side valley on the left and stay with the flow on a vague path across a wide bowl fringed by attractive rock outcrops until the steam reaches its source in a marsh. The faint path curves left round this, swinging south and continuing up a wide grassy groove – with an obvious rocky eminence appearing ahead – but about half a mile away. This is not Bessyboot but Rosthwaite Cam, so turn left onto the highest land and the cairn on the rocky little top of Bessyboot, AW's top of Rosthwaite Fell, will be quickly found.

A clear path winds down from Bessyboot towards Tarn at Leaves (indicating that most ascents of Bessyboot are probably from Rottenstone Gill and Borrowdale) but then a definite trod bypasses it and heads towards the square rock tower of Rosthwaite Cam, on higher ground further south. A fairly steep ascent soon leads to its flat top of naked rock, with a cairn, reached by an easy scramble from the back. It is a superb viewpoint, particularly to the north and west, but to the south the continuation of the ridge looks and is a complex mass of undulating high ground.

The descent from Rosthwaite Cam is into the basin of Great Hollow and a faint path leaves this to reach the third area of high ground on this broad ridge (the top of Cam Crag ridge), before descending to another wide depression. Combe Head, another shapely top on this broad ridge and one that can easily be mistaken for Glaramara itself, shows clearly now, beyond more hidden tarns and rough outcrops. As you make your way towards it, you will spot a curious patch of white on the rising fellside ahead; when reached, this proves to be an unusually large and almost completely solid slab of white quartzite. Just above it is a cairn on higher rocks and beyond that, also hidden from sight earlier, is the depression of Combe Door, where several tarns lie in an almost flat valley draining north-west to Combe Gill. Combe Head lies on the other side of this depression, and is defended by a belt of steep crags but they can be avoided by going left (south-east) and following a faint path up rough ground and then grass onto a little neck of land leading directly to the fine top and cairn of Combe Head itself. Overlooking Raven Crag, Combe Gill and Dovenest Crag with its huge land-slip caves, it is as good a viewpoint as Glaramara itself.

Glaramara now comes into view for the first time to the south, across a trackless depression holding half a dozen small tarns, but the obvious footpath rising from

Great End seen from the Glaramara ridge near High House Tarn.

Thornythwaite Fell, the trade-route up Glaramara, is soon reached and you can then turn left up it to the belt of crags at its base. A steep but easy 20-ft scramble (its polished rocks are a bit harder when wet) leads to some rock grooves and you then emerge between two rock points, either of which could be the summit, since there are cairns on both. The one to the left gives the best views, which are to Borrowdale, while that on the right has a windbreak at its base and is consequently a more commodious lunch-spot.

About 200 yards to the south-west, across a slight stony depression, is another cairn on an outcrop (which AW considered a second or twin summit) and the cairned path leads beyond it, with views to the sharp edge of Fleetwith Pike in the west. A short descent then ends down a stony gully beside low outcrops on the right and runs out onto a boggy hause (draining to Red Beck and Grains Gill) with a small tarn. A traverse of a higher, stony plateau beyond leads past an unnamed and beautiful tarn surrounded by low rocks, then a gradual descent leads to three more small ones (Lincomb Tarns) and a larger one, framed by rocks and with a little islet. This last one is High House Tarn and from here, as from the little one further back, there is a grand view all the way to Bowfell, its Great Slab clearly visible even across the distance. The views ahead, particularly those to the dramatic cliffs of Great End, improve with every step as you undulate over more rough ground, with two more separate little tarns, and then begin a longer, steady rise towards Allen Crags. A little more effort is needed to complete the ascent to the top, where several cairns are found amongst small outcrops. Despite sharing the same name as my own, honesty rather than modesty compels me to admit that this is not an exciting summit, as it is too closely overshadowed by its greater neighbours.

The obvious descent is on a good path to a four-sided windbreak on what is generally called Esk Hause (although that is strictly the slightly higher col at the head of Eskdale 300 yards south-west) and then turning downhill to the north-west on the well-worn track towards Sty Head. Reaching the head of Ruddy Gill, a well-used path turns off to the north-east, so take it but then immediately cross the gill and head for Sprinkling Tarn instead. There is no path, although a few sheep tracks help, as you contour along the east bank of this lovely tarn. Leaving it behind, undulating trackless land leads northwards with little change in height and, passing a couple of isolated tarns, make for an obvious large cairn, almost a beacon, seen ahead on a substantial rock outcrop. You have to dodge a quite large but almost overgrown tarn at its foot before you can scramble up to it, the generally accepted, and unjustly neglected, top of Seathwaite Fell. (There are other cairns that are slightly higher but on much less distinctive ground.)

Beyond the top, walk down steepening grassy fellside to the north, towards a vague rim of boulders and rocks, until the land drops away quite precipitously at Aaron Crags. These extend along almost the whole base of the fell but by trending right towards a noticeable buttress projecting furthest of all towards Seathwaite you will find a grassy gully immediately before reaching it. This gives an easy if steep descent of about 250ft,

Looking back to Great End and Seathwaite Fell from near Borrowdale Yews.

with one shaly bit in the middle, and easy grass slopes then lead down to a point where you can join the laid path (which used to be a river of stones) at the gate just before the last part of the descent to Stockley Bridge. A left turn here quickly leads to Seathwaite, where tasty teas may tempt you to linger awhile.

The final part of the walk uses the path signed on the map as the Allerdale Ramble. Turn right just before reaching the farm buildings at Seathwaite and a signed footpath leads you just outside the intake walls and down the east side of the valley. It is generally dry, almost all on the level and invariably peaceful: a delightful finish to a grand walk. Nearing Thornythwaite Farm the path is signed to bypass it, then the farm track leads to the road opposite Mountain View. Here, I am afraid, you must join the road but there is a gravel path alongside for much of the way and in only half a mile you turn right again and back to where you parked on the approach to Stonethwaite.

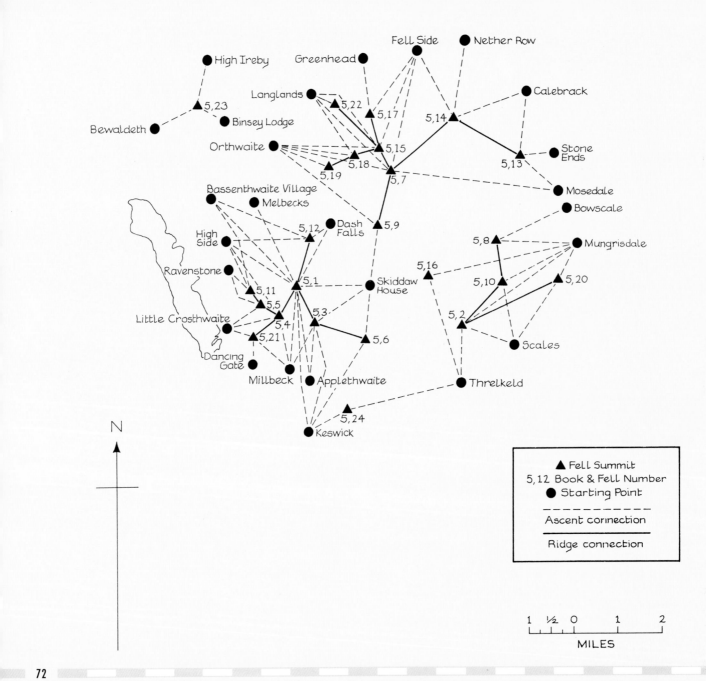

High Ireby

Greenhead

Fell Side

Nether Row

Calebrack

Langlands

5,23

5,22

5,17

5,14

Bewaldeth

Binsey Lodge

Orthwaite

5,15

5,18

5,13

Stone Ends

5,19

5,7

Mosedale

Bassenthwaite Village

Melbecks

Bowscale

High Side

5,12

Dash Falls

5,9

Ravenstone

5,8

Mungrisdale

5,16

5,1

Skiddaw House

5,10

5,20

Little Crosthwaite

5,11

5,5

5,2

Scales

5,4

5,3

Dancing Gate

5,21

5,6

Millbeck

Applethwaite

Threlkeld

5,24

Keswick

N

▲ Fell Summit
5,12 Book & Fell Number
● Starting Point
– – – – – Ascent connection
——— Ridge connection

1 ½ O 1 2
MILES

PART FIVE

THE NORTHERN FELLS

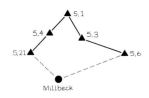

10 SKIDDAW AND LONSCALE FELL FROM MILLBECK

BEST MAP: *OS 1:25 000 Outdoor Leisure 4, North Western area*
APPROXIMATE TIME: *6 hours*
TERRAIN: *Dense conifer forest, open grassy fellside and shaly slopes. Footpaths are generally good.*

ITINERARY	Book & Fell No	Height of ascent	Distance of ascent	Cumulative distance	Height above sea level	
		feet	miles	miles	feet	mtrs
MILLBECK					400	122
Dodd	5.21	1250	1.50	1.50	1612	502
Carl Side	5.04	1075	1.50	3.00	2420	746
Skiddaw	5.01	780	1.00	4.00	3053	931
Skiddaw Little Man	5.03	190	1.00	5.00	2837	865
Lonscale Fell	5.06	175	1.50	6.50	2344	715
MILLBECK			3.50	10.00	400	122
Totals of heights and distances of ascent		3470	10.00			

Probably nobody but Alfred Wainwright would have noticed a ridge connection between Dodd and Carl Side. It is disguised even more by the fact that Dodd is almost entirely covered in forestry plantations while Carl Side and the other fells here are open and grassy. But the link is there and it makes possible a round that is both unusual and full of interest.

With Dodd at the start and Lonscale Fell at the finish of this particular ridge line, it is clear that the logical starting place is Millbeck which shelters under the tremendous northern slopes of Skiddaw. Don't park in front of the tiny village hall, however; instead drive west for a further 200 yards and you will find space for about five cars, just beside the sign pointing along the footpath of the 'Allerdale Ramble'. This path slants to the north-west across a brackeny fellside to the top of a larch plantation, then turns steeply

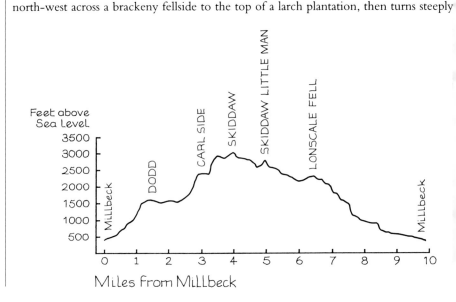

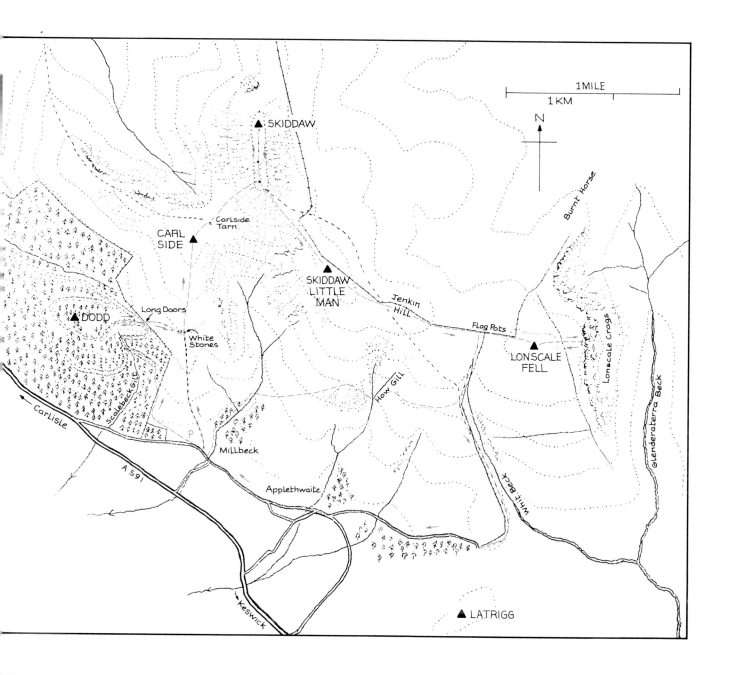

SKIDDAW

CARL
SIDE

Carlside
Tarn

SKIDDAW
LITTLE
MAN

Jenkin
Hill

Burnt Horse

Flag Pots

LONSCALE
FELL

Lonscale Crags

DODD

Long Doors

White
Stones

Scalebeck Gill

How Gill

Glenderaterra Beck

Carlisle

A 591

P

Millbeck

Applethwaite

White Beck

Keswick

LATRIGG

1 MILE
1 KM

N

uphill outside a strong wire fence, following the line of a collapsing wall and on the edge of a heavily afforested hillside. Seeing the massed array of tree trunks and having visions of finding the bones of missing Allerdale Ramblers gleaming palely amongst them, you shortly reach a step-stile attached to which is a yellow disc saying 'Forest Enterprise – walkers welcome here'. This is distinctly encouraging, particularly in view of AW's remarks that 'The climbing of Dodd is not to be achieved merely by repeating the process of putting one foot before and higher than the other … some crafty manoeuvring is required to reach the summit.'

Unfortunately, confusion follows immediately, for not only is it now difficult to follow AW's map, but on the other side of the stile I found two paths, one turning left downhill and the other turning right, uphill. There is no path going straight ahead. Downhill was no way to climb Dodd, so I turned uphill. Apart from uphill, this path has other things in its favour: it shadows the wall and fence on the right, you can see through the trees and its direction is right for the col of Long Doors, which both AW's map and the green pecks of the OS map suggest is a key point in the successful ascent of Dodd. It worked. Just as the path was becoming vague and the open ground on the edge of the forest to the right was disappearing I reached a level ride, heading north-west. In 100 yards it became a forest road, swinging leftwards in a curve to cross the tiny stream of Scalebeck Gill. (Just before the bend is what looks like a footpath continuing up a groove to the north-west. It is the right-of-way path, but be warned, do not bother with it: within 200 yards it is choked with fallen timber and brushwood.) A little way round the bend is a major junction of forest roads and, finding a forestry worker having a quiet zizz in his vehicle but who woke up as I approached, I established that I should turn sharp right here (due north). He also confirmed that it is a waste of time looking either for the old footpaths or trying to use fire-breaks to progress. So, following this firm wide track and heading due north, I climbed at an easy angle until it crossed Scalebeck Gill again. I ignored the choked-up line of the footpath – I could see where it *should* have gone – and continued (now heading east) to where it reached the forest fence, following it round sharp left to reach an obvious hause or col. This, it was plain, was Long Doors.

The Forestry Commission have for some reason given Dodd a very strange haircut, having run the clippers all round the crown but leaving a frizzy topknot of trees on the summit. The open area corresponds with the col of Long Doors, so there are wide, open views to Derwentwater and Keswick. Just over the top of the col is a smartly painted sign reading 'Dodd summit'. This too is a comfort. Following the sign, heading sharp back left (WNW) and upwards on a good gravel track, I reached another bend and another sign 'Dodd summit 300m'. Fortunately, it does not mean 300 metres of altitude, but it is the longest 300 metres I have ever walked. A well-used footpath winds a tortuous way through more timber and up a little rock scramble to reach the highest point of the fell. Here, overtopped by conifers, is not a cairn but a spike of slate set in a base, with a plaque and a Scout badge with the words: 'In memory of John Lole and Ian Sandelands 1st Seaton Scout Group 1980'. By jumping up and down, I could actually see Skiddaw Little Man, and from some nearby open ground found some long-range views along Bassenthwaite Lake.

(Having read about the 'crafty manoeuvring' needed to reach Dodd from Millbeck, I would have some sympathy if you decided it was not worth the effort. From the same parking place at Millbeck, just walk south-east along the road for about 100 yards and you will find a lane on the left and a sign reading 'Skiddaw Footpath' which will quickly lead you to the path leading directly up the ridge via White Stones to Carl Side. You will save about 300ft of altitude and about half a mile of distance.)

As I retraced my steps from Dodd to the col of Long Doors I was able to pick out clearly the line of the path through the heather towards the next top, Carl Side. From a stile on the col a footpath takes a rising traverse to the east to reach the obvious outcrop of large quartzite blocks appropriately called White Stones. (Ignore the green pecks on the OS map cutting off this corner: there is no path on the ground.) At White Stones, you join the south ridge of Carl Side and can follow either a fainter path directly up the ridge, or the main one which takes a slightly easier line. Carl Side is a wide grassy mound and its top is decorated by a small, slaty mound. Immediately beyond is the tiny puddle of Carlside Tarn.

From this junction an obvious path slants across the huge face of Skiddaw towering above, not taking the broad south-west ridge directly to the south top but trending left up an easier line. After rain, it is still like climbing wet slurry with slates sticking out, but

Lonscale Fell (centre) seen from Skiddaw's main summit, with the Dodds ridge in the background.

it leads to the summit ridge of Skiddaw, reaching a low circular windbreak on the middle top. Here firm ground is reached again, with splendid views over great distances. Turning left (north) a short stroll over slaty rocks leads down a slight depression and up to the main top with its concrete trig point, a triangular slate windbreak and a little pillar with a panoramic view indicator. Looking south-east, the continuation of the ridge to Skiddaw Little Man and Lonscale Fell can be seen.

Retracing steps to the middle top, a slight depression and gentle rise lead to the south top which is slightly lower but has a better viewpoint than the main summit. Then a wide cairned highway heads south-east, towards but avoiding Skiddaw Little Man, so it must soon be left in favour of a fainter path beside a wire fence which leads almost to its top. It is well worth the extra effort to reach it, for truly it is an independent mountain and unfortunate to be so named. But little men, it is popularly said, have big attributes. This one certainly has a distinctively sharp peak, commands a fine view back to Carl Side and has a superb prospect of Keswick.

The ridge continues, down and then up again, to the lower top of Little Man. Being smaller still, he has the biggest cairn, and this is stuffed with rusting iron fence posts, gesturing defiantly at Blencathra like a football fan. Just a little further down the slope you reach the main highway at a gate through the fence west of Jenkin Hill, but ignore the path and follow the line of the fence instead. You may spot the small low cairn in the grass on the almost flat top of Jenkin Hill but the fence remains a perfect guide across a wide depression, apparently called Flag Pots, rising to a corner where there is a gate. Beyond this more grass slopes rise gently to the rounded top of Lonscale Fell where there is a cairn; on my last visit there was a fence post stuck in it but such accoutrements have a tendency to come and go.

If that were all there is to Lonscale Fell you would feel cheated; all that grass for just a bit more grass and another poxy cairn! But Lonscale Fell has some surprises; you *must* continue as far as the east peak. Use a stile to cross a newer fence (not shown on AW's map nor the OS) and then walk over more grass to where it rises in a little lip and then suddenly ends. Now you are on the edge of the steep broken Lonscale Crags dropping 1500ft to the Glenderaterra Beck far below, a most dramatic contrast to the rolling prairie of the past half-hour's walking. You can see southwards down the long valley of St John's in the Vale, a major geological fault (*see* Great Calva 10), to the Dodds, Helvellyn and beyond, while to the north the crag-fringed Burnt Horse ridge curves towards Great Calva and the northern fells. Looking carefully below your feet you can pick out traces of spoil heaps, quarries and levels, for the lowest slopes of Lonscale Crags were mined for lead.

You now have to return to Millbeck. Go back to the top of Lonscale Fell and retrace your steps along the wire fence to the depression of Flag Pots. From here a faint but good path leads down the edge of Whit Beck to join the main Keswick–Skiddaw track. Now

here for a second or two and admire an exceptionally good view on the right to Bassenthwaite Lake.

The sharply defined ridge continues, with rough ground falling away on both sides and giving a view ahead, through the gap of Carlside Col, to Skiddaw Little Man and its precipitous slopes of rocks and scree. Scudding clouds and sunlight make a patchwork of shadows on the grey-green slopes of Skiddaw still rising impressively on the left; on the right you are looking down to Derwentwater and Keswick and to the tousled conifer-crowned top-knot of Dodd. And in no time at all you will traverse Longside Edge to the surprisingly large pile of slaty stones on the summit of Long Side itself.

This spot called forth one of AW's more purple passages. He describes how 'Its furnishings of fragrant vegetation – small soft carpets of dry mosses, bilberry and short heather: its quietness, airy elevation and glorious views make this one of the choicest of summits.' He was, as usual, right about the views, especially those back along the ridge towards Ullock Pike, and even the vegetation, despite the passage of many more boots, is still flourishing.

Your third top, Carl Side, is now less than half a mile away and requires only a very short ascent beyond the next depression to reach it. You will have to desert the path and trend right for a short distance to amble onto its broad and rounded top but you will not find a view worth looking at and so will soon stroll to the north-east and down to Carlside Tarn. This little puddle, for it is no more than that, is in reality far too small (20ft x 8ft, if that) to fit onto any map, even at 1:25 000 scale; I have been here in winter when it has been drifted over with snow and quite invisible as it has no depth and almost no vegetation on its margin. Nevertheless, lying here on this bare hause, dominated by the great slate spoil heap of Skiddaw still towering above, it marks a change, not only of direction.

The ascent of Skiddaw from here is an experience of a different kind. Avoiding the shifting slates and steeper angle of the broad south-west ridge (if you can call anything so ill-defined a ridge) the path now in normal use slants further left across the flank, heading north-east. It is mostly up a shaly scree of tiny slates and earth but in various places the underlying slabs of slate are exposed. Vegetation doesn't stand much chance here and upward progress is accompanied by slithering and sideways crab-like movements. I find this is the sort of slope on which my fashionable collapsible walking-stick (which I recommend so long as you are not too concerned with your 'image') is very useful as it provides a third leg on shifting ground or in high wind.

This path leads to the almost level summit ridge, which is nearly half a mile long, reaching it somewhere near its mid-point, at a low circular windbreak and cairn. This is not the main summit, although I have friends who, in a thick mist, once thought it was and then descended to Keswick. This was not such a silly mistake, for there is a slight descent from this point to the north, along the ridge, then continuing over shattered slate

The Ullock Pike ridge, seen from the path rising from Carlside Col to Skiddaw.

slabs and past several other small cairns. When you reach a large cairn, a windbreak and a trig point, you can be certain that nobody would bother to build all these things unless it were the true top of Skiddaw.

Interestingly, AW did not provide a view indicator for Skiddaw, as he did for almost all other tops, preferring in the case of this mountain to do several drawings instead. For those who still prefer an indicator they will find one actually erected here, on a pedestal near the trig point.

Continuing about 200 yards further north, still almost on the level, you reach another large cairn marking the north top, then a gentle slope leads downhill towards a depression, rising again onto the wide grass-and-shale top of Broad End (incidentally the second

Broad End on Skiddaw, the other, southern one, being between Skiddaw and Little Man). On the descent, a backward glance will show a few slabby rocks facing down Barkbethdale which are distinguished by the name of Gibraltar Crag; on Scafell you would not even notice them. There are numerous cairns on Broad End but they do not indicate a path nor mark its highest point so it is difficult to imagine their purpose. There is, however, a wire fence in good repair which crosses the northern Broad End from near Skiddaw Little Man and this provides an infallible guide for the continuing descent towards Bakestall, whose little top is now seen lower down the slope. A path on shale and scattered slates and then on grass beside the fence leads to a surprisingly large cairn about 100 yards off to the north of the continuation of the path. Why build a cairn here, you may wonder; this insignificant top is only a pimple on the backside of Skiddaw. Only when you have looked back up from below will you appreciate that it crowns the extensive crumbling mass of Dead Crags, above the waterfall of Whitewater Dash.

The descent and final return remain to be completed. The most obvious route, but longest and involving most tarmac, is to complete the descent of Birkett Edge beside the fence to the north-east, turning left on the path (becoming a tarmac track) below Dead Crags, reaching the Orthwaite road again almost opposite Peter House Farm. An alternative would be to reverse AW's ridge route in Bakestall 4, using a heather and grass spur between the edge of Dead Crags and Dead Beck, but this is very steep and very little used. The third way is surely the true continuation of the ridge northwards from Skiddaw over Broad End, descending to Melbecks over the little fell of Cockup – not to be confused with either Little or Great Cockup to the north-east. AW was not very encouraging about this, saying that 'Probably this line of approach to Skiddaw is never used from one year-end to another.' He also says that a gate and hurdle have to be climbed which are surmounted by barbed wire. 'Long legs are needed to avoid mishaps. Ladies have shorter legs than men, and should mind their bloomers.' Fortunately this situation has changed and there should be no ripped knickers or anything else nowadays.

Leaving Bakestall, therefore, down fairly steep grassy slopes to the north-west, cross the deep gill of Dead Beck fairly high up where it is shallow, then a slight rise on grass (passing a couple of swampy pools) leads to a heap of stones on top of Cockup. Then, going west off the top, head for the obvious line of Cockup Gill; a wall and fence to its right run down the fields (north-west) towards the farm at Melbecks. The public path runs to the left of the wall and fence, and a normal gate (not barricaded) gives access to it. This leads down to a gated farm track which shortly reaches the Orthwaite road on a corner. Following this round to the left will lead back to the start in just under a mile. If you fancy a rural ramble to finish instead, follow the sign (just before reaching the road) for High Side and then paths do lead via Hole House Farm and farm buildings at Barkbeth. But be warned; it is very little used, much more complex than it appears on the OS maps and cows have pushed signs over. I would sooner stick to the road.

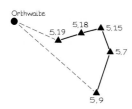

12 DASH BECK'S NORTHERN SKYLINE

BEST MAP: *OS 1:25 000 Pathfinder 576 Caldbeck. Alternatively OS 1:50 000 Landranger 90, Penrith, Keswick & Ambleside area.*
APPROXIMATE TIME: *5 hours*
TERRAIN: *Mostly over rolling grassy fells on fair paths, at times giving harder going than you might expect. There are some quite boggy sections.*

ITINERARY	Book & Fell No	Height of ascent	Distance of ascent	Cumulative distance	Height above sea level	
		feet	miles	miles	feet	mtrs
ORTHWAITE					800	244
Great Cockup	5.19	950	2.00	2.00	1720	526
Meal Fell	5.18	300	1.00	3.00	1770	550
Great Sca Fell	5.15	460	0.75	3.75	2131	651
Knott	5.07	250	0.75	4.50	2329	710
Great Calva	5.09	480	1.50	6.00	2265	690
ORTHWAITE			3.75	9.75	800	244
Totals of heights and distances of ascent		2440	9.75			

If you want to avoid the crowds on a busy weekend, these northern fells can still be guaranteed to provide an escape, an opportunity to stretch your legs and fill your lungs with good fresh air. The surprise of this circuit is the inclusion of Great Calva.

Turning off the A591 Keswick to Carlisle road, a narrow minor road signed for Orthwaite curves to the north-west around the northern end of the Skiddaw massif. The start of the walk is a public bridleway (grid ref 253337) and it is possible with care (and without blocking any gates) to park a few cars on the verge between the farm at Orthwaite and the one at Horsemoor Hills. This public bridleway is a good track, partly tarmac, leading roughly south-east towards Brocklecrag Farm, but in a quarter-mile turn off left (finger-post) onto a fine grass pathway slanting gently towards the top of a slope where outcropping white quartzite boulders and blocks make Brockle Crag so distinctive. (The name 'Brockle' seems particularly appropriate, a hint of speckled badger.) Across

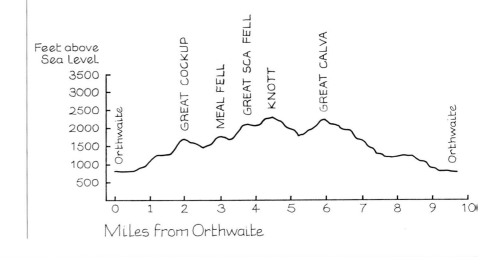

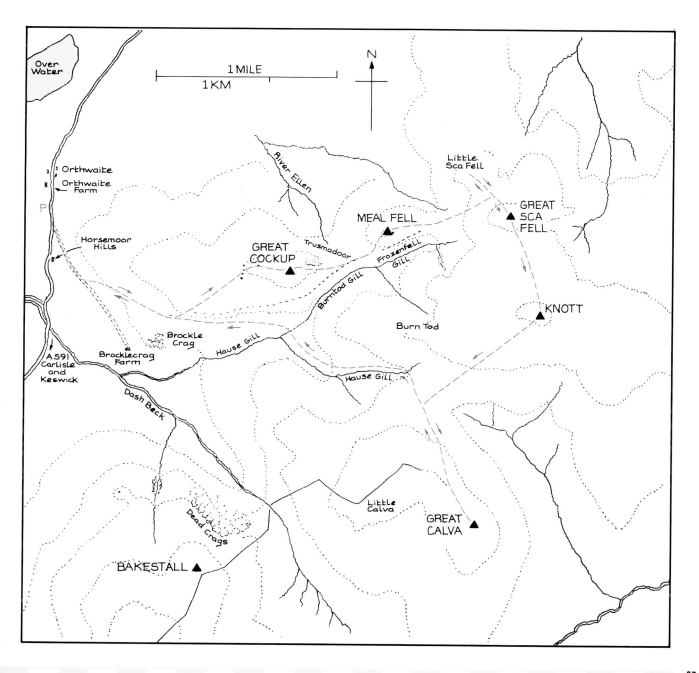

Over Water

Orthwaite
Orthwaite
Farm

P

Horsemoor
Hills

Brockle
Crag

Brocklecrag
Farm

A591
Carlisle
and
Keswick

Dash Beck

Dead Crags

BAKESTALL ▲

River Ellen

Trusmadoor

GREAT
COCKUP ▲

Burntod Gill

Hause Gill

Hause Gill

Little
Calva

GREAT
CALVA ▲

1 MILE
1 KM

N

MEAL FELL ▲

Frozenfell
Gill

Burn Tod

Little
Sca Fell

GREAT
SCA
FELL ▲

KNOTT ▲

87

the valley of the Dash Beck, on the right, the downfall of Dead Crags, receiving almost no sunshine, forms a huge dark shadow on the fellside below Bakestall and the long slope above leading to Skiddaw.

About a hundred yards above and north of Brockle Crag the path becomes indistinct on the ground, but a fairly small and isolated round boulder, just above and left of the line of the bridleway, marks where a grassy trod leads uphill to the north-east. (I do not think that this is the boulder shown by AW on his map, which is perhaps a quarter-mile further east.) This faint path heads for another boulder seen on the skyline but then fades into grass, bilberry and heather slopes which lead to the first of several circular stone-built grouse-butts. A last short climb leads you to a prominent cairn on the west end of the broad ridge of Great Cockup. This looks as if it should be the summit, but about 300 yards further east is a much smaller cairn and it certainly looks to me as if this one is on the highest point. From here, the views are dominated by Skiddaw, but in the mornings they are likely to be backlit outlines with little detail.

A path to the north-east leads down a grassy groove and then swings a little to the right to trip lightly down a slaty edge with scree falling on the left of it, reaching the pass of Trusmadoor at its foot. AW called this 'a perfect pass ... what a place for an ambush and a massacre!' Looking north through this curious gap, you get a long view towards flatter lands drained by the River Ellen, while the eroded flanks of Burntod Gill, stretching to the south-west from here, provide a frame for more views to Broad End and Dead Crags.

The next top of the ridge is Meal Fell, on the other side of Trusmadoor, and a tempting broad grass path rises across its flank, above the waters of Frozenfell Gill, encouraging the hope that the top will be somehow reached more easily by using it. Not so, I'm afraid; you can use it for a couple of hundred yards, but will then have to accept that it was built for farmers or miners but not peak-baggers, and turn up the untracked grassy slope on the left to reach the top of Meal Fell. From Great Cockup you would have seen what looked like a prominent outcrop of stones on its top, but when you arrive the 'outcrop' proves to be a large circular stone windbreak, much more substantial than you might expect, with other rocks nearby. These are complemented by a few evil ponds in an adjacent fold of land.

An easy descent now leads you to a broad col above which the slopes of Great Sca Fell rise steeply, rather too steeply for a comfortable ascent. The top of Great Sca Fell is, however, a very indefinite sort of place and its cairn is a miserable sort of effort on the top of a wide and broad dome. In short, it is a place which you can easily lose, or miss, or cross without knowing you have ever been there. In mist, I have done all three. On the other hand, the cairn on Little Sca Fell (which is to the left of the col between the two) is vastly bigger and there is a sort of sunken stone windbreak next to it. It has a superior view, and is altogether a better place to visit and to find. So don't go flogging

Looking down Frozenfell Gill to Great Cockup from Great Sca Fell.

up that steep grass slope in front of you; instead, follow a faint path which slants up the left flank of Great Sca Fell to reach the col mentioned above. Now you can turn left in the certainty that you will find the big cairn on Little Sca Fell and *then return* to the col, on a footpath which, as is only proper, links the Little with the Great. Doing this, you are certain to locate the fiddling little cairn on Great Sca Fell and will know that you are going in the right direction for the next top on the ridge, which is Knott.

After crossing a very broad depression, which is not particularly boggy, a steady rise up a slope to the SSE, which at times *is* especially boggy, leads towards Knott. The path

Looking south-east back to Hause Gill from Brockle Crag, with Burn Tod on the left.

is fairly distinct, running out onto a rounded top where patches of close-cropped grass alternate with circular-shaped areas of shaggier appearance, suggesting that the sheep are very discriminating about which kinds they will have for lunch. A few stones form a cairn on the open and exposed top from where there are extensive views, lots of fresh air and sky, but not much to photograph.

When you are standing on Knott, and even more when you are shortly descending the path that leads from Knott to the south-west, you could make out a good case that 'the ridge' now leads westwards along Burn Tod. AW decreed otherwise. The ridge routes go to High Pike (no use to us today), to Great Sca Fell (been there already) and to Great Calva. Well, it's a lot better objective than Burn Tod. From Knott, Great Calva is unquestionably the nearest shapely mass of interest, a broad dark pyramid to the south, its top just level with the distant but distinct edge connecting Lonscale Fell and Skiddaw Little Man. So that's the way we go.

A narrow but clear path leads south-west towards an obvious col at the head of Hause Gill, giving a grassy descent at an easy angle. Once reached, a right-angle turn to the south-east leads across the northern flank of Great Calva, using a path which crosses some very juicy land. If your boots are not well greased, the juice will be leaking from your seams for five minutes after reaching dry ground, found (more or less) on the broad top of the ridge at a line of (wire-less) fence posts. The posts lead towards Great Calva, although they give out before reaching it, and a last pull leads to the stony summit where there is a large cairn and a windbreak on the eastern slope. However, this dilapidated structure would now hardly be described as a 'splendidly-constructed windproof shelter', and the other one, found 150 yards south along the ridge with two more cairns, is not much better. Safer to rely on good windproof clothing. A feature of the view from here is the long line of sight along the geological fault (which AW called The Great Central Fault, *see* Great Calva 10) through St John's in the Vale to Windermere (also seen from Lonscale Fell), but Carrock Fell and Skiddaw are also well seen.

Retracing steps to the col between Great Calva and Knott (having tiptoed delicately again over those juicy bits) you now turn downhill to the west, down Hause Gill. The top part of this is a steep-sided ravine, surprisingly stony on its flanks but with a good path threading down it. The path crosses the beck two or three times on slaty footing but very soon continues down the quiet valley to the junction with Burntod Gill. From here the gently rising line of a green path, clearly visible even through summer bracken, leads to a traversing footpath towards Brockle Crag again. Do trend left off the path and walk the very short distance to have a closer look at the quartz outcrops; if you have time to spare, you could also have a quiet sit-down with a grand view back to the rolling fells you have just crossed.

All that remains is to traverse a bit of fellside to pick up the bridleway path back to Orthwaite.

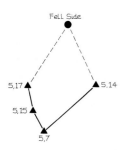

Fell Side

5,17 ▲   ▲ 5.14

5,15 ▲

▲
5,7

13 THE DALE BECK SKYLINE

BEST MAP: *OS 1:25 000 Pathfinder 576 Caldbeck. At 1:50 000 scale Landranger 90 Penrith, Keswick & Ambleside area.*
APPROXIMATE TIME: *4½–5 hours*
TERRAIN: *Some good paths and tracks; otherwise over rough grass, heather, and a few boggy areas. Not advisable in misty conditions.*

ITINERARY	Book & Fell No	Height of ascent	Distance of ascent	Cumulative distance	Height above sea level	
		feet	miles	miles	feet	mtrs
FELL SIDE					950	290
Brae Fell	5.17	1150	2.50	2.50	1920	586
Great Sca Fell	5.15	270	1.00	3.50	2131	651
Knott	5.07	250	0.75	4.25	2329	710
High Pike	5.14	380	2.50	6.75	2157	658
FELL SIDE				2.50	9.25	950	290
Totals of heights and distances of ascent		2050	9.25			

Dale Beck drains the heart of the Caldbeck Fells and its deep ravines still show the evidence of the widespread and very productive mining operations that took place here. This ridge walk traverses the high land around the headwaters of Dale Beck, giving some good tramping and fine views.

The start is the little hamlet of Fell Side, a couple of miles south-west of the attractive little town of Caldbeck, and cars can be parked at the side of the metalled track next to the entrance to Fellside Farm (grid ref 304374). From here, walk south-east along the remaining bit of tarmac and turn right through a gate at its end, finding a sign just round the corner that reads 'Footpath Roughton Gill and Caldbeck Fells', which confirms that you are at least starting from the right place. A good gravel track now leads south, shortly passing a disused gravel pit on the left, and allowing intriguing views ahead to the south-west of Brae Fell and the two Sca Fells, Little and Great. Shortly afterwards,

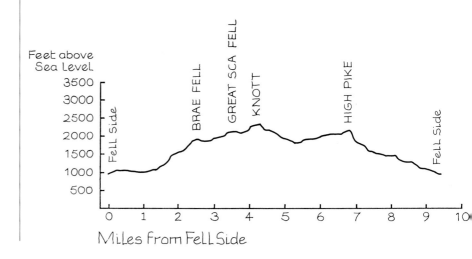

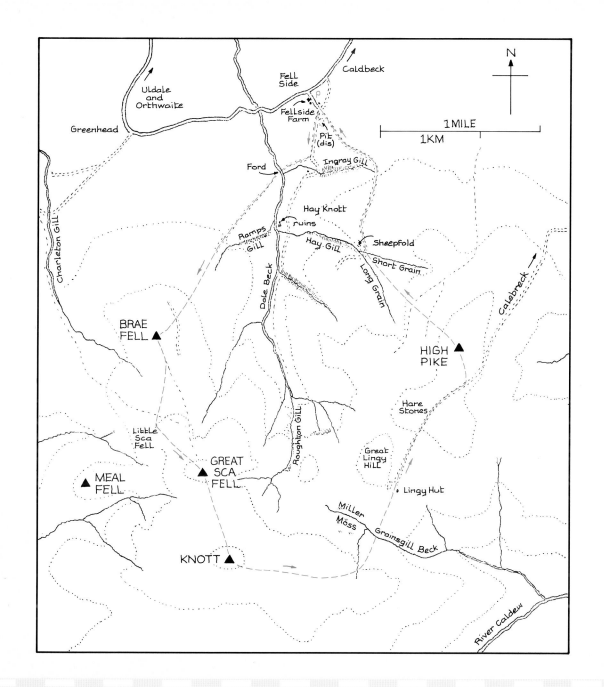

N

Caldbeck

Fell
Side

Uldale
and
Orthwaite

Greenhead

Fellside
Farm

Pit
(dis)

Ford

Ingray Gill

1 MILE

1 KM

Charleton Gill

Hay Knott

ruins

Ramps
Gill

Hay Gill

Sheepfold

Short Grain

Dale Beck

Long Grain

Calebeck

BRAE
FELL ▲

HIGH
PIKE ▲

Roughton Gill

Hare
Stones

Little
Sca
Fell

Great
Lingy
Hill

MEAL
FELL ▲

GREAT
SCA
FELL ▲

Lingy Hut

Miller
Moss

Grainsgill Beck

KNOTT ▲

River Caldew

the track kinks into Ingray Gill and across the bend can be seen a small square building, a water treatment plant for North West Water. Before reaching the bend, turn downhill to the right on a grassy tractor track beside a little stream which leads to a ford across Dale Beck. If the water-level is low you can cross dryshod easily; if it is not so low you can try the 'quick-dash system' by which you try not to let either foot stay long enough in the water for any of it to get into your boots – and I wish you luck. If it is high, and you cannot bear to get your tootsies wet by taking your boots off altogether, you should walk upstream for half a mile to where there is an easier crossing near the bottom of Ramps Gill where there are some ruins of old mine buildings. (This is AW's advice, incidentally.)

Assuming you do cross at the ford, you have the benefit of a tractor track heading WSW up a broad grassy slope as far as the head of Ramps Gill, but then it fades away into the grass. This leaves you with no alternative but just to tramp up the rest of the slope. If you have enough breath, you might try whistling a cheery tune to keep your pecker up. You will cross a transverse bit of track but do not allow it to divert you from the uphill task and you will shortly reach a large cairn with a small, circular windbreak next to it in a rash of stones. This is Brae Fell; and that was the worst part of the walk over.

From having no footpath at all, an obvious one now materialises as you leave the cairn and head just east of south along it. However, by sticking with this path (sheeptrack?) it is clear that you will miss a very prominent cairn silhouetted on the nearest high land, so after about a quarter of a mile you will naturally follow a footpath trending rightwards off the track towards the cairn. It soon fades in tussocky grass and you then have to make your own way once more over a last bit of rough land. Just before the final rise you will cross a grooved path rising from Charleton Gill which also avoids your intriguing cairn, so continue on the steep grass which leads you to your goal, at last. This, you feel, ought to be Great Sca Fell. It has a fine cairn and a grand view and a sunken windbreak next to it – but it is Little Sca Fell which is not an AW top. Fortunately, the real thing is not far away.

Once again, a quite clear path leads from the cairn, to the SSW and down a slight depression, then rising uphill again (and almost disappearing en route) onto a broad, grassy, rounded mound where there is a very small cairn. *This* is Great Sca Fell. It is nowhere near as impressive as Little Sca Fell, but it is a few feet higher. One has to wonder where, in all these acres of grass, the stones for the cairn came from. You can stride out now, on a peaty path over more grass, across another slight depression – which is, in fact, an important watershed, separating the River Derwent from the River Eden – towards Knott, whose broad hump looms ahead like an elephant's back. There is some wet and slutchy ground on the rise, but then the path almost disappears again as it runs out onto firm ground with areas of close-cropped grass. Knott's summit cairn is located in the middle

of a circle of gravel. By strolling north a hundred yards or so you will be able to look down Roughton Gill and other fine ravines scoured out and ravaged for their minerals.

From Knott, the next and last main top is High Pike, to the north-east. The direct route does not look too attractive as a wide expanse of peat groughs and drainage channels intervenes. A check on the map discloses that the area is named Miller Moss, which deepens your suspicions.

However, a broad ridge extends to the east, a wide spur of land with Grainsgill Beck on the north side and the River Caldew on the south and this spur looks as though it will give you an opportunity to skirt round the morass. A faint path leads down the spur but it is not reliable and soon disappears in tussocky grass. It then reappears as you swing left, north-east, aiming for a strange, square box-like structure, looking from a distance rather like an Elizabethan half-timbered house, and standing out very prominently on the south-eastern slope of Great Lingy Hill. This faint trod turns down the line of a

From the slopes of High Pike looking over Roughton Gill and Dale Beck to the Brae Fell-Great Sca Fell ridge.

shallow gill, crosses the head of Grainsgill Beck – with a fine view down the valley beyond towards Mosedale – and then reaches firm ground again where it becomes a good path.

The 'box' is soon reached and you realise that the Tudor appearance is because its exterior is clad in black roofing felt secured by light-coloured timber battens. It is called the Lingy Hut, it is water-tight, has open access, and would be a good bivouac spot. A notice inside it advises that it is maintained by the Lake District National Park, that over a thousand people use it each year and would you therefore leave it in good order. Some idiot has obviously tried to light a fire on the wooden floor, scorching it. There is also a visitors' book and, as usual, a few interesting entries. One, by a girl, read: 'After sleeping here last night we are cold and tired and will appreciate a nice fire. Beware of the dirty old pervert who knocked on the hut at 2 a.m. asking for a light.' It's amazing what goes on up there, isn't it?

From the hut, which incidentally has a sheepfold just above it on the fellside, a firm, broad track leads just east of Great Lingy Hill (although I could only see tussocky grass on its summit) and passes over the round hump of Hare Stones. Here there is a large cairn next to the track, with a much smaller one on slightly higher land on the left, on point 627m. A slight depression follows, then the track swings away across the eastern flank of High Pike, heading for Calebreck. You leave it and turn up the slope on a clear path and soon reach High Pike.

There is a surprising amount of stone on the top of High Pike. There is, in consequence, a huge cairn and a semi-circular windbreak. There is a trig point and a seat made from two solid pieces of slate with plaques on the seat in memory of Mick Lewis, who died in 1944 aged only sixteen years, and of his mother who died in 1970. Fifty yards to the north is yet another cairn and ten more yards beyond that two walls are still standing of what AW tells us was a shepherd's cottage. What a situation! Nettles grow against the inner wall, nettles in ruins like this being a sure sign of human habitation. I doubt if there are any other nettles within several miles. The views from here are outstanding, with a grand one back over Roughton Gill to Great Sca Fell.

On leaving, head north-west down pathless grass slopes onto the broad tongue of land between the two gills of Long Grain and Short Grain which join at the tip of the tongue to form Hay Gill. On the way you will cross two tracks, one just a faint trod and the other the old miners' path linking Nether Row with the Roughton Gill mines. Just before reaching the tip of the tongue, swing left and cross Short Grain to the remains of a sheepfold and an obvious track. This track rises gently to the north-west across the broad moor ending in Hay Knott, curves rightwards round a small boggy basin and then trends downhill again, just east of north. It crosses the head of Ingray Gill, where there is the first squelchy passage for some time, then turns north-west again to Fell Side. It joins the outward route just above the disused gravel pit that you passed on the outward journey and all that remains is to turn through the gate again back to the car.

From the head of Grainsgill Beck, looking east towards Mosedale.

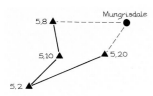

14 THE GLENDERAMACKIN ROUND

BEST MAP: OS 1:25 000 Outdoor Leisure 5, North Eastern area plus Pathfinder 576 Caldbeck. At 1:50 000 scale, OS Landranger 90 Penrith, Keswick & Ambleside area covers the whole walk.
APPROXIMATE TIME: 5 hours
TERRAIN: Mostly straightforward walking over grassy fells on reasonable paths. The Sharp Edge alternative ascent to Blencathra is a rock scramble.

ITINERARY	Book & Fell No	Height of ascent	Distance of ascent	Cumulative distance	Height above sea level	
		feet	miles	miles	feet	mtrs
MUNGRISDALE					750	229
Souther Fell	5.20	950	1.25	1.25	1680	522
Blencathra	5.02	500	2.50	3.75	2847	868
Bannerdale Crags	5.10	200	1.50	5.25	2230	680
Bowscale Fell	5.08	250	1.25	6.50	2306	702
MUNGRISDALE			2.25	8.75	750	229
Totals of heights and distances of ascent		1900	8.75			

For most fellwalkers the highlight of this splendid circuit will be the ascent of Blencathra by Sharp Edge. But even if the very idea of something called *Sharp Edge* gives you the willies – and it horrifies some of my own friends and relatives – the alternative ridge of Scales Fell is just as valid a route to the top, without the apprehensions.

The walk starts from Mungrisdale, reached in a couple of miles north from the A66, and there are a few places to park by the village hall opposite the Mill Inn (grid ref 363303), or on the verge just before reaching it. The long ridge of Souther Fell rises directly behind the inn and AW described a direct approach to it which has since been banned. To outflank the walled fields which you cannot legally cross at present, go over the footbridge

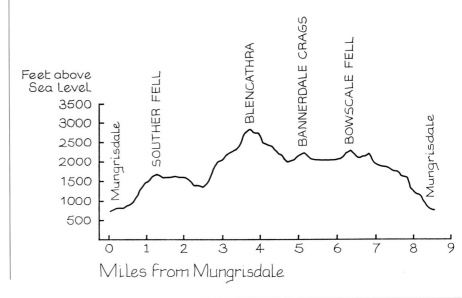

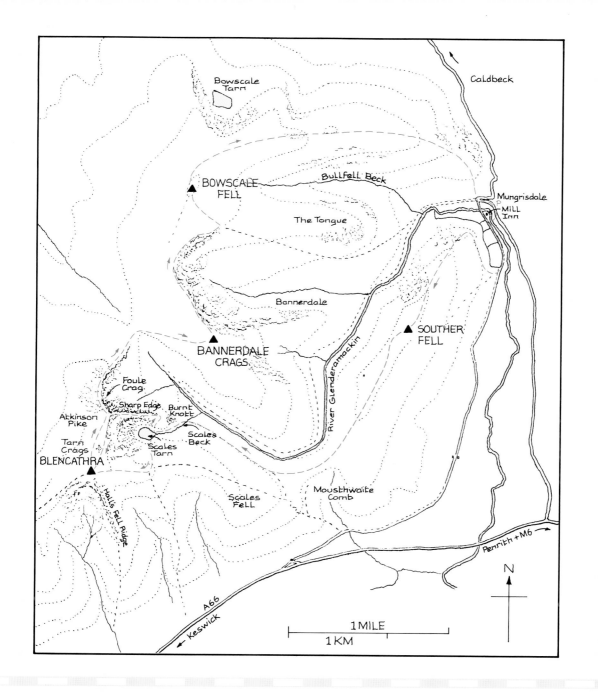

Caldbeck

Bowscale
Tarn

Bullfell Beck

▲ BOWSCALE
FELL

The Tongue

Mungrisdale
MiLL
Inn

Bannerdale

▲ SOUTHER
FELL

▲ BANNERDALE
CRAGS

Foule
Crag

Sharp Edge
Burnt
Knott

Atkinson
Pike

Scales
Beck

Tarn
Crags

Scales
Tarn

BLENCATHRA ▲

Halls Fell Ridge

Mousthwaite
Comb

Scales
FeLL

River Glenderamackin

Penrith + M6

A66

Keswick

N

1 MILE

1 KM

to the inn and then turn left (south) along the back road beside the river. In about 300 yards you reach a fell-gate and beyond it can turn back sharp right, outside and above the intake wall and fence, and soon pick up a path leading to the end of the spur directly above the pub. From here a grassy path rises sharply between a few outcrops and then up the grassy ridge at an easier angle – although I guarantee you will still be puffing – until you reach a long whaleback ridge with a couple of humps on it. The nearest seems to be Souther Fell's summit and a tiny slate outcrop seems to relate to the OS spot height of 522 metres/1713 feet, so it has risen over 30 feet since AW was here. There is quite a good view to the cirque of Bannerdale Crags with the top of Blencathra just peeping over the intervening ridge.

Temporarily leaving the main line of the march along the top of the fell, a definite trod leads out to a well-built cairn, which is perhaps a beacon since it seems to be on a line of sight between Penrith and St John's in the Vale. A slight descent follows to the col at the head of Mousthwaite Comb, where the River Glenderamackin is deflected to flow north, and Blencathra comes much more fully into view.

But before leaving Souther Fell (also called Soutra Fell) for Blencathra I must mention the fascinating story of what AW calls 'The Spectral Army of Soutra Fell', *see* Souther Fell 7. In this he describes how on midsummer's eve of 1745 a group of twenty-six people all attested how they had seen soldiers, horsemen and carriages moving in an unbroken line along the top of the fell and over steep ground that the observers knew was impossible for them to negotiate. On checking the following morning, for the procession continued until nightfall, they could find no trace whatsoever of the visitors. To complement this weird story, W. Heaton Cooper, in his book *The Tarns of Lakeland*, mentions that the name 'Blencathra' means 'hill of the devils' and suggests that this is because 'a form of mirage has been observed on the mountain', the best known of which are the three which lasted for several hours on the midsummer eves of 1735, 1737 and 1745 when great numbers of horsemen and carriages were seen to be moving at great speed across the steep face of the mountain and then to disappear. This additional material suggests that both Blencathra and Souther Fell were involved in these ghostly visions.

From Mousthwaite col an obvious path traverses the side of Scales Fell to the north-west, on the left bank of and above the River Glenderamackin, making for the fine outline of Sharp Edge. In a little over half a mile a cairn marks where the path forks; take the left-hand fork, which turns uphill beside the turbulent Scales Beck. This path shortly crosses to the right bank on big stones and then leads uphill over a rise to the edges of Scales Tarn. This is situated in a glacial bowl and the long slopes of scree falling from Blencathra's heights and from the crags of Sharp Edge on the right create a most dramatic arena for it.

With Sharp Edge now in view, if you are dithering and not sure what to do next,

Peter Linney on Sharp Edge, on the slab just before the notch.

this is a good place to rest and consider. Have a Mars Bar, have a sandwich, have something to drink. While you do I will describe the 'ordeal' ahead, possibly the hardest of the regular walkers' routes in the Lakes.

Although generally known simply as 'Sharp Edge', this ascent is in fact made up of two parts. Sharp Edge itself is a gently rising crest of rock which drops away steeply on both sides and is made up of a form of black slate which is not friable or crumbly but weathered into larger blocks. It ends at a notch, beyond which rises Foule Crag, a steeper and quite broad incline of slaty rocks which merges into the summit slopes.

To begin the ascent, a slaty path climbs up the slope above Scales Tarn, quickly reaching the lower part of the Sharp Edge ridge above Brunt Knott, then turning left along it. A choice of ways is soon presented: for the most direct, simply scramble up broken rocks to reach the crest and then generally follow it all the way up, enjoying the exhilaration of the drop on each side, until it reaches a slightly tilted and polished slab just before the notch. Alternatively (as with Striding Edge on Helvellyn), you may avoid the crest by following a footpath on the right-hand side, about thirty feet below the crest, but when it ends you must climb some slaty steps to join the crest at the tilted slab mentioned above. In windy or otherwise poor conditions the footpath is obviously easier.

Crossing the slab is best done by taking a couple of bold steps across it (there is no good handhold) and stepping into the notch beyond; alternatively a shuffle on one's bottom may be found less nerve-racking – how did you imagine the slab became so polished? You think you've now cracked it, but Sharp Edge, although providing the most spectacular part of the ascent, is not really the problem. The trickiest bit, after stepping out of the notch on its other side, is in moving rightwards across some sloping rock and into a series of grooves on Foule Crag, up which you now go. After about forty feet, the grooves fade into easier runnels, soon reaching an obvious footpath across grass which curves southwards above Tarn Crags to reach the highest point of Blencathra. Under dry conditions, the ascent is straightforward; when wet, iced or very windy the difficulties are obviously greater and the exposure can be intimidating.

It is worth mentioning that it is very unusual to *descend* by this route, mostly because it is more awkward to do so but also because of the immense problems that would be caused by parties trying to pass each other.

If dithering whilst sitting at the edge of Scales Tarn has turned into a decision to avoid Sharp Edge, the next stage is simply a series of steps up an obvious steep path leading from the left edge of the tarn to the Scales Fell ridge above. This has developed over the last twenty years or so and shows that plenty of other walkers were here before you. Just follow it uphill and you will reach Hallsfell Top. For me, the best view from here, in the right light, is that looking back over Scales Fell and Souther Fell.

The next top is Bannerdale Crags, so head off north down a shaly, mossy slope to a tiny tarn in a little depression, then continue past a large cross made up of quartzite stones embedded in the ground (perhaps to ward off the devils?) to a large cairn on Atkinson Pike which crowns the rocks of Foule Crag, above Sharp Edge. A slaty path now curves to the north around the edge of the cirque of Foule Crag and descends about 700ft to the hause where the River Glenderamackin rises. Two paths fan out from here, one going left, the other heading east towards the highest point on the, as yet unseen, rim of Bannerdale Crags. This is the path to take and, although it fades on the last rise, you will soon spot the high cairn of slaty black rocks on the top, close to the edge of the fine cirque of broken rocks and steep ground. There is a good prospect of lonely Bannerdale and a fine view down a spur to the north-east, with Souther Fell again in sight.

There are traces of old lead mines at the foot of Bannerdale Crags and you may spot them as you follow a good path around the rim above, but this path turns sharply right at the far end of the cirque and then slants down the flank of The Tongue into

Looking south-east towards Souther Fell from Bannerdale.

Bannerdale. That path would curtail the walk and give a quick return if necessary, but assuming otherwise leave it before it begins its descent and steer a north-westerly course across trackless grass and quickly pick up another path climbing more grass slopes to the NNE. This will soon lead to a circular stone windbreak on the top of Bowscale Fell, the summit cairn being at the same height and 100 yards further north. There are no decent views from here but it is a pleasant place on a warm day. The ridge now descends slightly to the north-east, towards a minor depression beyond which there is a further gentle rise to a cairn on the east peak of Bowscale Fell. Before turning up the slope to this, a short diversion of fifty yards north will disclose Bowscale Tarn far below, for years reputed the haunt of two immortal fish.

From the east top, descend the east ridge. It is at an easy angle over grass and bilberry, with a path showing on blue slate shale here and there and with a good retrospective view of much of the route. A steeper descent at the end, with the path winding down through gorse, emerges at the foot of the fell beside a small quarry and opposite a large building of classical-looking architecture; a notice on its door describes it as the Post Office. I cannot see it surviving privatisation.

A left turn here on a grass track leads to a gate and the road in a further fifty yards. The road goes round the corners of several fields but a signed footpath cuts the corner and down some steps to finish directly opposite the Mill Inn again.

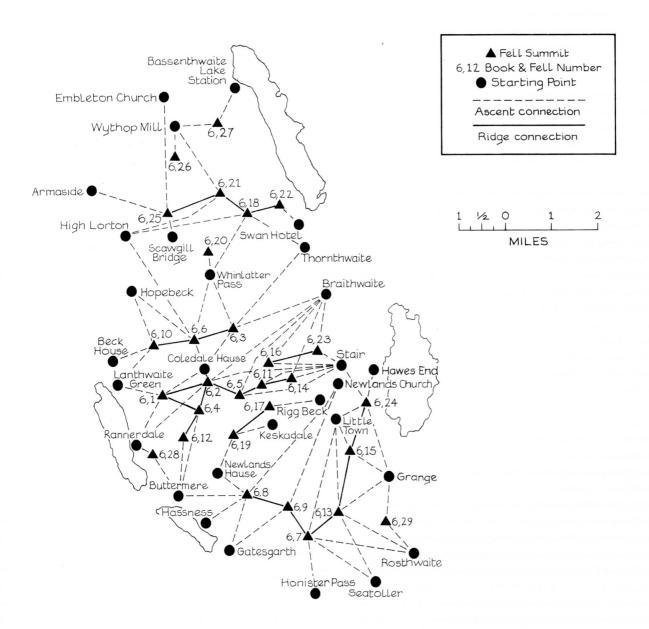

PART SIX

THE NORTH WESTERN FELLS

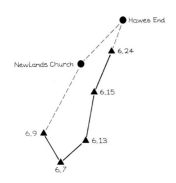

15 THE COMPLETE NEWLANDS BECK SKYLINE

BEST MAP: *OS 1:25 000 Outdoor Leisure 4, North Western area*
APPROXIMATE TIME: *6–6½ hours*
TERRAIN: *Almost all on good paths over firm ground.*

ITINERARY	Book & Fell No	Height of ascent	Distance of ascent	Cumulative distance	Height above sea level	
		feet	miles	miles	feet	mtrs
HAWES END					300	91
Catbells	6.24	1250	1.50	1.50	1481	451
Maiden Moor	6.15	720	1.50	3.00	1887	576
High Spy	6.13	300	1.50	4.50	2143	653
Dale Head	6.07	900	1.50	6.00	2473	753
Hindscarth	6.09	250	1.25	7.25	2385	727
NEWLANDS CHURCH			2.50	9.75	650	198
HAWES END			2.25	12.00	300	91
Totals of heights and distances of ascent		3420	12.00			

This splendid circuit begins with the ascent of Catbells, which AW rightly called, 'One of the very best of the shorter climbs. A truly lovely walk.' It continues as a high-level traverse, giving grand views over Derwentwater and Borrowdale as well as down the valley of the Newlands Beck itself, before descending the delightful ridge from Hindscarth to Scope End. There is a re-ascent to Dale Head in the middle of the walk but great improvements to the path have made this much easier than it used to be.

The ridge of Catbells terminates at Hawes End (AW spelled it Hawse), with a clearly defined nose that gives an obviously attractive way of ascent. The best place to leave a vehicle is in the Gutherscale car parking area, on the wide bends of the road there (grid ref 247211). Just beyond the cattle-grid, between the two main bends, is a notice erected by the National Trust asking that the signed path be used to prevent erosion. This is to discourage walkers from the original route, which used to go straight up the steep lower slope of the nose directly from the cattle-grid; however, it is also to deter them from using what AW called the 'enchanting stairway' of Woodford's Path. This is a series of zigzags starting from an old green road on the left (E) side of the nose and which

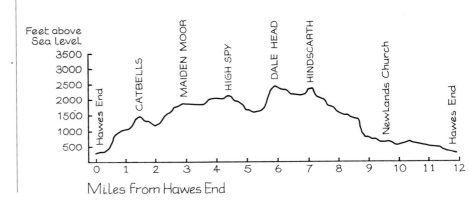

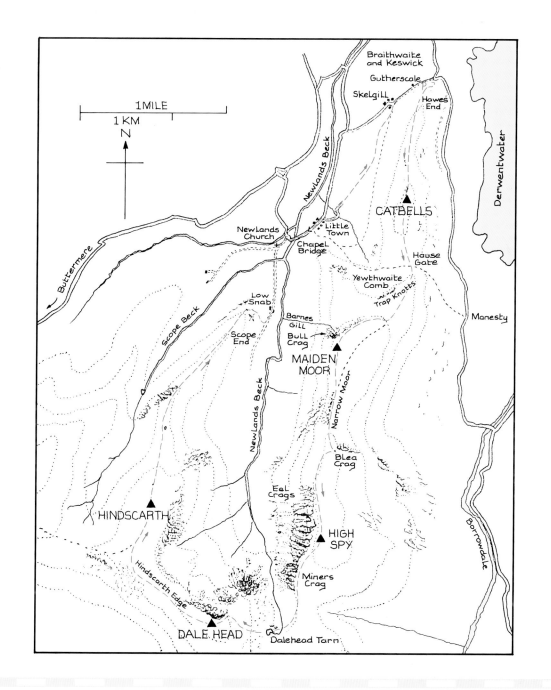

originally gave an almost effortless ascent up its lower part, until over-use almost destroyed the path completely. Happily, the re-routing is succeeding in allowing the scars to heal nicely but at the time of writing it is still fenced off.

The newer, good shale path is signed up and across the right side of the nose to the top of the first steep section and then zigzags upwards from one side of the ridge to the other. It shortly reaches a little outcrop of slate where there is a plaque set into the rock commemorating Arthur Leonard, the founder of Cooperative and Communal Holidays, who died in 1948. He could not have had the foggiest idea of how many people would now walk past his memorial.

A short rise above the outcrop the path leads to a first summit, with a little depression just beyond it from where, across the slope to the right, towards Newlands Beck and Little Tarn, you may spot the spoil-tips of the old Yewthwaite Mine. Another gentle rise up the ridge, past two more minor depressions, leads to an easy scramble up a staircase of slaty rocks on the final steeper tower. The top of Catbells, of brownish rock with numerous little pockets which tend to hold tiny pools of water, is reached immediately beyond, giving a fine view across the fields of Newlands to the prominent top of Causey Pike and the other Derwent fells.

Descending the slope beyond Catbells you will notice a black hole, of the terrestrial not the astronomical variety, on the south side of Yewthwaite Comb, where a mine shaft or adit was driven into the fellside of Trap Knotts. Then the broad col of Hause Gate is reached, which is crossed by a well-used path between Little Town and Manesty, once in regular use by miners. A straightforward climb follows up a rather long rise on a broad path to where the angle eases noticeably on the edge of a wide plateau. The broad path continues ahead, but it is simply linking the shortest distance between two points and ignoring the most interesting views; it also bypasses the highest point on Maiden Moor, the next top. So leave it here and tend rightwards along the edge of the escarpment to reach the fine blunt-ended Bull Crag, sharply defined by the steep grassy gully of Barnes Gill and overlooking the Newlands valley again. It is a notable viewpoint from which you can look down to the rifts of the Goldscope Mine at the far end of this horseshoe walk, look back to Catbells along the ridge and, as you leave it and continue along the rim to the south, get an unexpected view to Great Gable through the gap between Dale Head, on the right, and the summit of High Spy, on the left.

The next landmark is a fine cairn, seen ahead but well before you come to High Spy, and it is reached as you rejoin the main path and follow it along the firm edge of Narrow Moor, with crags dropping away on your right. The cairn is on the prominent rock outcrop of Blea Crag and you just turn off the path for a few yards to the left to visit it. The reward is a splendid view along Derwentwater while, looking back towards Maiden Moor, the alternating grass and heather bands running down the fellside look like a zebra's flank.

Leaving the cairn on Blea Crag, a short descent follows to a depression, then the main ridge path climbs gently again, becoming narrower and more rocky but gaining little extra height as it leads towards a tall and well-built cairn on High Spy. On the way, it passes above the gullies and broken cliffs of Eel Crags which tumble in confusion towards Newlands Beck, giving more grand views across the upper Newlands valley to the great bulk of Dale Head, the next main top on the round. But another notable sight from here is that of an astonishing sweep of exposed slate slabs on the eastern flank of Hindscarth. From this viewpoint they look so obvious, yet when you are walking along the broad

High Spy (left) and Dale Head, seen from Eel Crags.

back of Hindscarth itself, as you will be doing shortly, they are completely unseen and forgotten. The views from the cairn on High Spy, while extensive to the south towards Great Gable and the Scafells, are restricted by being rather far back from the edge of the crags, so it is unlikely that you will be hopping about with your camera here.

Dalehead Tarn, lying in the depression linking the two halves of this circuit, although partly shielded by two rock outcrops, is visible to the south on the stony descent from High Spy towards the head of Newlands Beck. A cairned path leads towards it, passing above more steep cliffs on Miners Crag, to reach a crossing-point of Newlands Beck itself, just above a place where it splashes through a little gorge. A causeway of flat stones now leads over boggy ground beyond, climbing to reach the tarn itself where a couple of little sheepfolds shelter behind the larger of the two rock outcrops that help to contain it.

This is a natural place to pause, whether for a sandwich, a pee or just to take stock of the awful-looking ascent that lies ahead up a steep and dreary slope which looks from here as if it is mostly scree and boulders. My previous memories of this ascent have been of unrelieved toil made worse by much slithering backwards, so that the 800-ft-plus height gain felt more like 2000ft. AW obviously had similar experiences, describing this ascent as 'rough, steep and tiring' and saying that it was much easier to make a long loop left to join the path coming up from Honister. Since I had my chum Trevor Waller with me on this particular walk I proposed that he take AW's leftward loop route while I took the slope direct. Neither of us would walk at other than a normal pace and we would leave Dalehead Tarn at the same time.

I set off expecting a hard time but found to my surprise that the old loose and horrible path is now a beautifully pitched stairway almost all the way up the slope, to as far as a little shoulder on Dale Head and after that it was easy walking on grass and shale up the edge overlooking the steep crags on the right. Some of these steep crags are called Great Gable but are not, of course, to be confused with *the* Great Gable of Wasdale. Because of the tremendous improvement to the path it was a far easier ascent than I had expected and so, although I had been keeping up a steady pace and consequently arrived at the top like a clockwork beetroot, I was there at least five minutes before Trevor. He had been battered by sudden wind and rain but said there were good views towards Borrowdale. Whilst waiting, I sat beside the superbly built cairn on the highest point, sheltered from the squall and admired the views at my feet down the Newlands valley and across to Eel Crags and High Spy.

The hard work is now over as you leave Dale Head and go westwards along the ridge towards Hindscarth, the next top. A short stretch of generally level if rocky ground leads to a descent of Hindscarth Edge to a grassy hause, passing isolated fence posts on the left where the ridge is quite narrow; from here there are good views to Fleetwith Pike, Honister, Pillar and Great Gable. From the hause a now well-established shaly path

The trod along the crest soon rejoins the main path and leads on along the level to a grassy hause where there is a tiny tarn, no more than 12ft long and almost filled by grass and vegetation, lying just left of the path. Approaching this hause, it becomes perfectly clear that the slope rising above leads directly to Hindscarth and the appearance given below, from near Newlands Church, that it is a detached mountain is an illusion. There are some striking quartz-tipped rocks at the foot of the slope and then the path climbs up flakes of rock and shale interspersed with more lumps of quartz, the last pull being up a steeper slope leading to a substantial cairn hollowed out into a windbreak at the top.

There was a time, a summer's day not so many years ago, when I carried my then young son up this last slope from the tiddly tarn on my shoulders. Nowadays he is almost strong enough to carry me. I also recall one winter's day when these upper slopes were completely iced over. I had not really been expecting ice and had only popped a pair of four-point instep crampons (originally designed for walking on gently inclined Austrian glaciers) into my rucksack at the last minute. I should have put them on earlier than I did and so teetered about and did not secure one of them properly. Just as I was on the steepest and nastiest bit of ice only a short way from the top, I realised that one crampon was about to come off my boot and had to make a couple of desperate shuffling movements to ensure that I did not lose it. I then almost crawled up the last rise to the cairn.

As *you* stroll up here on a fine day, it will be difficult to imagine such conditions. But there is no doubt that, for me at least, some of the most memorable days that I can recall on these wonderful hills have been those when the conditions were unfavourable. The spice of a little danger made it seem all so much more worthwhile and enjoyable – in retrospect.

Wandope, Eel Crag and Sail, with Grasmoor behind, seen from Robinson's north-east ridge.

This windbreak/cairn is in fact the best viewpoint on Hindscarth, with a grand panorama to Wandope, Eel Crag and Sail in particular, and the windbreak provides unusually good shelter for a short rest for a swig from your flask and a honey butty or two, but please take your orange peel with you. A gentle rise only then remains to reach the main summit cairn a couple of hundred yards further along this broad top.

About a quarter of a mile after leaving the summit cairn and heading south, the paths split on the stony ground and you need to trend right to reach the path along Littledale Edge, from where you get a sudden sight of Buttermere and the deep defile of Honister Pass. The remains of a few old iron fence posts mark the way along the edge of a shallow escarpment as far as a grassy hause. After that, the fence is largely intact and it accompanies you on a steady pull up the far slope, firstly on grass and then through a belt of shaly rocks, then more grass to a large cairn at the top. From here you look over to Crummock Water and Loweswater, to Rannerdale Knotts and Grasmoor. It is also the point at which you need to leave the fence and swing right (N) to follow a cairned, shaly path up a very slight rise to reach two low outcrops, like ledges, of very distinctive reddish-grey rock with quartz bands. Here you will find the summit cairn of Robinson and a fine view to Eel Crags.

As on Hindscarth, a gentle descent along the broad ridge north-eastwards leads to another prominent cairn at the top of a steep descent, also with a fine view down the ridge beyond; the difference this time is that although the path leads down a broad slope, it is edged on the left by the very steep ground of Robinson Crags, which gives an exhilarating sense of exposure as well as tremendous views. This north-east ridge of Robinson, particularly in its upper part, is rather like the crest of a breaking wave rising gently from green grass slopes on the right and then tumbling over a crest of light-grey rocks, like foam, towards Keskadale Beck far below. After the initial swoop downhill, there is a little step with a few rock outcrops, then easier ground before a sharp descent on rocks towards an elegant grassy ridge seen beyond. The rocks are shaly, sloping and rather polished and much care is needed if they are wet or iced. Halfway down, assuming you are feeling relaxed enough to look, you will again spot that little reservoir in the ravine below on the right.

A second rock step follows almost immediately afterwards, down the edge of Blea Crags, and it is unseen until you have reached it. This is noticeably more awkward than the step above as the angle of the rock is even more inclined outwards and its surface is more polished. There is no disgrace – sturdy trousers or breeches permitting – in resorting to some bum-slithering here to reinforce the friction of your boots, but you can avoid this section altogether by skirting round it to the left. After that, there is just one small rise over a last outcrop on Blea Crags and then the path continues along the lovely turf of the slender ridge of High Snab Bank, a gentle descent made even more delightful by the lovely views ahead to the Newlands valley.

Almost at the end of the ridge and with the intake wall in sight, a finger-post signs a permissive path to the right down a long, grassy slope with pocketed footsteps to reach a farm track. A left turn through the gates here leads past the buildings of Low High Snab and a tarmac track completes the descent to Newlands Church and the car park.

Looking down the north-east ridge of Robinson towards Newlands.

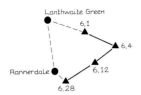

17 THE RANNERDALE ROUND

BEST MAP: *OS 1: 25 000 Outdoor Leisure 4, North Western area*
APPROXIMATE TIME: *4½–5 hours*
TERRAIN: *A steep ascent, initially over scree and then up rocky ground, followed by easy high-level walking and a fairly steep descent on good paths.*

ITINERARY	Book & Fell No	Height of ascent	Distance of ascent	Cumulative distance	Height above sea level	
		feet	miles	miles	feet	mtrs
LANTHWAITE GREEN					500	152
Grasmoor	6.01	2300	1.50	1.50	2791	852
Wandope	6.04	160	1.25	2.75	2533	772
Whiteless Pike	6.12	110	0.88	3.63	2159	660
Rannerdale Knotts	6.28	220	2.00	5.63	1160	355
RANNERDALE				0.75	6.38	350	107
LANTHWAITE GREEN				1.50	7.88	500	152
Totals of heights and distances of ascent		2790	7.88			

However improbable it may seem, especially if you are looking up at Grasmoor from Lanthwaite Green, this circuit linking Grasmoor with Wandope and Whiteless Pike is a logical and exhilarating horseshoe walk around the skyline of Rannerdale Beck. The faint-hearted will be intimidated by the obvious initial steepness of the direct ascent but, as is so often the case, the sense of achievement is that much greater when you have had to make a bit of an effort. It is certainly one of my own favourites on these north-western fells.

Next to Lanthwaite Green Farm, at the north end of Crummock Water, is a large layby (and telephone) which is the best place from which to start (grid ref 159207). Before setting off, however, it is as well to study the ground ahead; flogging steeply uphill in

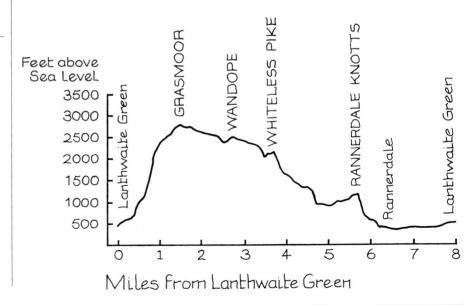

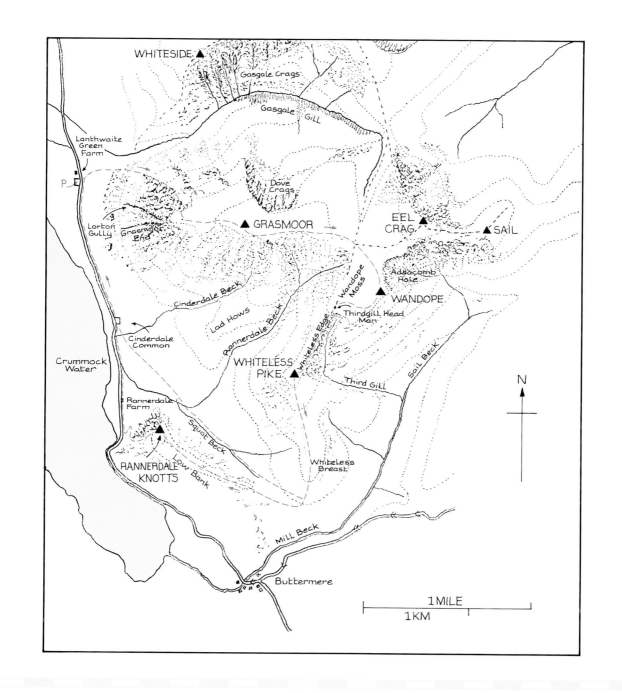

the wrong direction is a *very* unrewarding experience. Seen from here, the huge face of Grasmoor (which AW called 'a formidable object') is riven by many gullies but by two in particular which form an inverted 'V'; the left-hand one is Lorton Gully. To the left of these gullies, the crags turn an obvious corner, forming a very broad nose, into Gasgale Gill and the route essentially goes up the line of the nose. A path leads from the layby up a broad and gently angled grassy spur (with bracken in summer) to a lower belt of scree and the light-coloured scar of a path can be clearly seen and traced through this towards the crags of the nose.

The hard work begins once you reach the scree and the path zigzags up it and then up grooves through a zone of tough heather until you have gained about 400ft from the grassy spur below and you reach an obvious rock gateway formed by two broken buttresses. Going through this, then curving rightwards beyond it, you quickly reach a short, slanting, grass-and-heather gully or steep rake and at its top emerge onto a wide terrace. Instead of fighting your way uphill with your head down, you can now start to enjoy the route. You can even relax for a minute and appreciate good views across Crummock Water to Mellbreak, to Darling Fell and Blake Fell and across Gasgale Gill to Whiteside.

From the top of this rake there is now an apparent choice of ways, either to left or right along the terrace. Neither are of any use. There are many signs of traffic on the terrace going to the left but I suspect this is because many feet have chosen that way but then returned back along it, for it quickly fades into sheep-tracks below steep crags which lead towards Gasgale Gill. Going to the right along the terrace is soon found to lead towards another wide belt of crags on the main face: not an attractive option. Only one way remains (apart from the unthinkable one of down) and that is directly up, up a couple of easy rock steps (trending slightly leftwards) and then up more easy rocks above, towards a large rock pinnacle seen ahead. Incidentally, AW called the bit immediately above the terrace 'Fat Man's Agony'. He should be so lucky; I never found anything that gave *me* much of a squeeze here. You continue on the edge of a shallow gully on the left and then join it to its top. Once there, you find that the flat top of the large rock pinnacle is just on the right, giving a fine belvedere with more grand views. Here you can rest and reflect that if you ever thought you were going to face insurmountable difficulties on this route they are now all behind you. You can also see that you are now just a little below the height of Whiteside and so must be at about 2000ft. That leaves about 800ft still to go.

From here the continuation of the route can be seen to be a curving arête or ridge and at an easier angle. It begins with a short ascent (only about 6ft) up little rock ledges and the ridge curves firstly to the left and then to the right, with a path winding over rocks and through heather up its edge. It emerges from the steep ground, about 400ft above the pinnacle, at a cairn on a grassy shoulder on Grasmoor End and quite clearly

Looking from the top of Grasmoor over Whiteless Pike to Buttermere, the Scafells and the High Stile ridge (right).

now slightly higher than Whiteside. There is a bigger cairn about 100 yards further on, then the last bit of the ascent is up easy-angled slopes on a grassy and then shaly path to an untidy, multi-chambered windbreak on the top of Grasmoor. That's it: you are up and you can feel pleased with yourself. I suspect AW had his tongue in his cheek when he said that 'On the whole, however, the climb is probably less difficult than the north wall of the Eiger'. This is the highest point, but better views are obtained from another pile of stones about 200 yards to the south-east, overlooking Crummock Water.

The summit area of Grasmoor is a big plateau, about half a mile long and tilted to the east. The most used path leads east from the viewpoint cairn along the rim to reach another large cairn. Just beyond it, only 50 yards away, a glance down the slope to the right will show where the Lad Hows Ridge curves steeply down towards Crummock Water. Cross the plateau at its narrow waist, heading due north from here if you wish to take a peep down the tremendous combe of Dove Crags, but otherwise continue on the obvious path to another large cairn at a point marking where a steeper descent leads down to the grassy col between Grasmoor and Eel Crag (*see* page 124).

Two well-marked paths lead from here, one eastwards up a well-cairned slope to the top of Eel Crag and a second, heading SSW, cuts across the grassy Wandope Moss. You don't especially want to visit Eel Crag today and the other path avoids Wandope. Worse, t completely misses the sight of Addacomb Hole, whose rim is immediately below the summit of Wandope, so make your own way to the south-east up a gentle slope to the cairn on Wandope's grassy top and have a look down this fine hanging valley.

Continuing south-west along the ridge-top towards Whiteless Pike, the path strides confidently along, leading gently downhill and overlooking the fine valley drained by Sail Beck and Mill Beck below. Whiteless Pike can be seen rising at the far end of a narrow ridge which looks interesting and clearly must be traversed, so you press on towards it. Then you realise that the path is veering sharply off to the right towards another large cairn and may wonder why. The cairn is Thirdgill Head Man and it is at the head of a rapidly deepening ravine (Third Gill) filled with sharp-edged boulders, scree and little waterfalls. If you fail to veer out to the cairn, you will quickly find that you are on a false ridge and not heading for Whiteless Pike but making a rather precipitous descent to the valley.

From the cairn, a rocky ridge leads downhill to the south-west, sharpening to form the fine crest of Whiteless Edge. This gives an exposed and exhilarating traverse, with no awkward steps or other difficulties, as far as a little col beyond which it rises upwards to the elegant summit of Whiteless Pike. AW graced it with the alternative name of 'the Weisshorn of Buttermere'.

From the summit, the ridge does in fact continue in a direct line to the south-west (and I have descended it without difficulty in the past to the lower part of Rannerdale Beck) but it is steep, rocky, heathery – and pathless. For all of the above good reasons, therefore, the normal route of descent (which is the way AW recommended anyway) is on a clear path down the steep grass slope southwards towards Whiteless Breast. The gradient eases as the path swings right and then briefly steepens again to reach a depression at the head of Squat Beck (which is also the head of Rannerdale).

AW's route leads directly back to Buttermere village from here but, unless you have arranged a lift, you will need to return to Lanthwaite Green. There are two options. Firstly, you may turn right (north-west) and follow the good path down the valley between the ridge of Low Bank and the vast slopes rising back up to Whiteless Pike and Grasmoor. If you do this, switch to the north bank of Squat Beck at a footbridge as you reach the intake walls and you may then follow the path easily to where it joins the road beside Crummock Water at Cinderdale Common.

Secondly – the way that I prefer because it enables you to stride another fine ridge and gain an additional Wainwright top with very little extra effort – slant away from the valley path and rise slightly to gain the grassy crest of Low Bank. This rises very gently, with views down to Buttermere village below, to where rocks thrust above the turf and then a delightful stretch of an almost level and often rocky crest leads to the cairn on the highest point above the crags of Rannerdale Knotts. Here the path turns sharply

Whiteless Edge and Whiteless Pike seen from near Wandope.

downhill to the left to avoid the steep rocks and descends to a shoulder, finally turning back right below the rocks to join the road below.

Whichever route you choose, a walk back along the line of the road is now unavoidable. However, for much of the way it is possible to tramp along the softer ground of the right-hand verge and you will enjoy some lovely views across Crummock Water as you go.

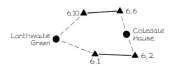

18 THE GASGALE GILL HORIZON

BEST MAP: *OS 1:25 000 Outdoor Leisure 4, North Western area*
APPROXIMATE TIME: *5–5¼ hours*
TERRAIN: *On good paths for much of the way, although an optional section traverses some rough ground and all direct descents from Grasmoor are steep.*

ITINERARY	Book & Fell No	Height of ascent	Distance of ascent	Cumulative distance	Height above sea level	
		feet	miles	miles	feet	mtrs
LANTHWAITE GREEN					500	152
Whiteside	6.10	1850	1.50	1.50	2317	707
Hopegill Head	6.06	360	1.13	2.63	2525	770
COLEDALE HAUSE			0.75	3.38	2000	610
Eel Crag	6.02	850	1.00	4.38	2749	839
Grasmoor	6.01	450	1.25	5.63	2791	852
LANTHWAITE GREEN			2.00	7.63	500	152
Totals of heights and distances of ascent		3510	7.63			

This walk along the best ridge in the north-western fells gives an exhilarating high-level traverse and then works its way round to Grasmoor via Eel Crag, with a wonderful opportunity to climb AW's 'Tower Ridge' en route. The descent from Grasmoor is no less exhilarating than the start and the whole walk gives connoisseurs an opportunity to sample some of AW's less obvious routes on these splendid fells. The name 'Eel Crag' may cause some confusion. AW was adamant (*see* Eel Crag 2) that 'Eel Crag' is the correct name for the major fell which the OS have named 'Crag Hill', and for that reason the name Eel Crag has been used throughout this book. Matters are complicated further because the north-east slope of this fell, overlooking Coledale Hause, consists of a steep and rocky downfall with several buttresses; this is called Eel Crag and gave its name to the fell as a whole.

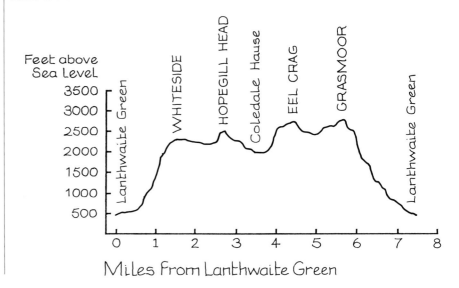

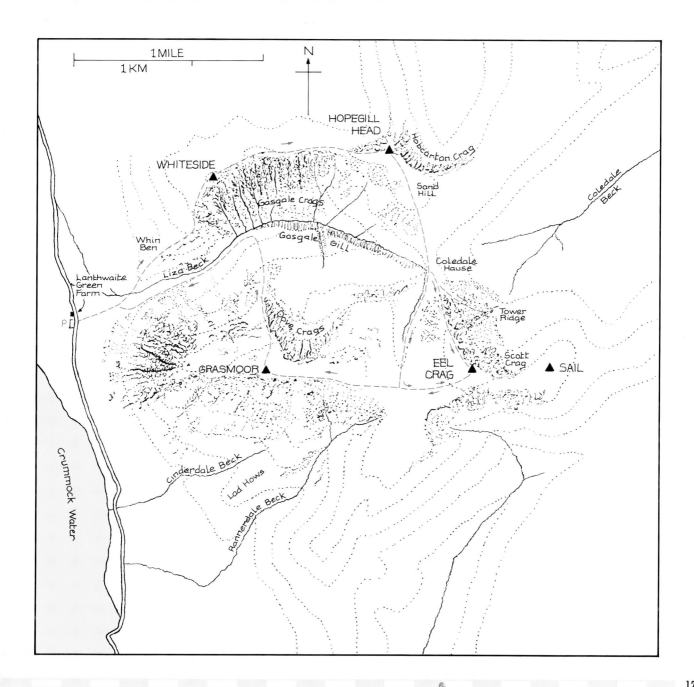

HOPEGILL
HEAD

Hobcarton Crag

WHITESIDE

Gasgale Crags

Sand
Hill

Coledale
Beck

Whin
Ben

Gasgale Gill

Liza Beck

Coledale
Hause

Lanthwaite
Green
Farm

P

Dove Crags

Tower
Ridge

GRASMOOR

EEL
CRAG

Scott
Crag

SAIL

Crummock Water

Cinderdale Beck

Lad Hows

Rannerdale Beck

N

1 MILE

1 KM

There is a purpose-built layby next to Lanthwaite Green Farm at the north end of Crummock Water (grid ref 159207) which is the best place to leave a car. From here a green path leads north-east (through tall bracken in high summer) towards the obvious defile of Gasgale Gill. When the path forks, keep on the left branch to reach a footbridge across the Liza Beck. As soon as you are on the other side, do not take the main path turning right up Gasgale Gill but climb the short, steep bank above, using some pocket steps, to reach a green path rising towards the minor top of Whin Ben. The lower slopes are clothed in bracken and the higher ones in heather and the path climbs up a groove through these and over exposed rock to reach the level top of Whin Ben, beyond which more slopes lead towards Whiteside. A short climb leads to a little shoulder overlooking Gasgale Gill and then the angle steepens noticeably and the path climbs up some slaty rocks for a short way before reverting to scree on the last easier-angled stretch.

Just before reaching the top a peep over the edge on the right discloses the great mass of shattered shaly rocks riven by deep gullies which form Gasgale Crags. The top of Whiteside itself is a little upthrust of shaly rock with a few scattered stones but what immediately catches the eye is the ridge now stretching eastwards towards Hopegill Head, with a secondary and probably higher east top about a quarter of a mile away; splendid walking is promised. Looking from this vantage point across to Grasmoor on the other side of Gasgale Gill, it will be seen that the north flank of Grasmoor had a great bite scooped out of it by ice to expose the steep but vegetated buttresses and gullies of Dove Crags. The right-hand edge of the scoop (as seen from here) is well defined and will provide the eventual route of descent.

An obvious path now undulates along this lovely ridge, mainly over grass and shale, but the most interesting part is the last section where it rises towards Hopegill Head. This is in two tiers and on the first of them the ridge sharpens into a rock crest for a short way before reverting to shale on the second tier which rises to the splendid pyramid summit of Hopegill Head. This is at the apex of three ridges and offers a particularly interesting view eastwards along the rim of Hobcarton Crag towards Grisedale Pike, but the next top on this round is Eel Crag, to the south, beyond Sand Hill.

There is a slight descent before a small rise to the rounded top of Sand Hill, then a slope which is partly grass and partly rather loose shale leads to the wide and grassy crossroads of Coledale Hause. On this descent, it is well worth studying the lie of the land ahead to decide which variation you will choose of the routes to Eel Crag (the fell). The *direct* route is clearly defined by the right-hand edge of the crags and steep ground facing left (north-east) down Coledale and this is the true ridge-line. In clear visibility and good conditions, it leads up a short scree slope (or via a once grassy rake) and then scrambles with no difficulty at all (and with several variations) up grassy ledges and rocks to easier ground, following a line of cairns which lead to the trig point on Eel Crag.

In poor visibility, or most particularly under ice and snow when complete winter

Looking back towards Whiteside from the ridge near Hopegill Head, Gasgale Gill on the left.

equipment is highly advisable, this normally obvious and simple route can be quite awkward. Then the *safest* route is to locate the path beside the stream, the infant Liza Beck, which flows down the shallow valley between Eel Crag and Grasmoor. This path leads upstream (SSW) as far as a junction on an unnamed hause, where there are a couple of tiny pools. You then turn east up a grass slope to follow a cairned path to the trig point on Eel Crag.

The third alternative, the most *adventurous* route, is to gain Eel Crag by way of what AW called Tower Ridge because of its slight resemblance to the great ridge of the same name on Ben Nevis. But before any reader, or my editor, starts having palpitations I will also quote AW's own comments about this: 'It is necessary in a few places to handle rocks but there is nothing to cause fear or panic, although ladies in ankle-length skirts may find odd places a little troublesome.' My good friend Harry Sales, who is well over seventy and has a plastic hip, enjoyed it greatly.

So for Tower Ridge, which is to be found round the corner on the left overlooking Coledale, start on the direct route, by a sketchy path up the scree to where it runs into a shallow gully cutting through a belt of rock, but then traverse left and onto the face looking down Coledale. Continue traversing across some rather tiresome scree to reach a well-defined two-stepped rock ridge in a splendid situation in the middle of a great cirque. The ascent of the ridge, during which about 350ft of height is gained, is obvious and straightforward, with good rock and even an arrow scratched on a slab. When steeper rock seems to bar the way, a little ramp, slanting bottom left to top right, provides the key and then the rock runs out onto an easy grass ridge soon connecting with the rim of the sloping plateau above. A left turn (south) soon leads in about 100ft of ascent to the trig point. Nearby there is a little seat fashioned from a few flat stones, and views overlooking Scott Crag and the ridge towards Causey Pike.

Grasmoor is the next top and a line of cairns runs down the grassy slope from the trig point, WSW, to the hause between Eel Crag and Grasmoor (the reverse of the *safest* route described above) and then a rather too obvious cairned path climbs the slope to the west towards Grasmoor. This reaches a large cairn at the point where the slope joins the plateau. The plateau is about half a mile long and generally quite broad although it narrows in the middle where the rim of the cirque of Dove Crags cuts into it. There are several paths on the plateau but the best-defined one continues along the left (south) edge, passes another big cairn marking where the Lad Hows ridge curves down between Rannerdale Beck and Cinderdale Beck and then continues to a large, multi-chambered windbreak on the highest point on Grasmoor. The views to the south and west are extensive, but even better from a smaller shelter on the nearby edge overlooking Crummock Water, where a tremendous panorama extending to the Scafells can be enjoyed.

Looking for a way off Grasmoor, which is a cul de sac, is somewhat like walking the plank: there appears to be plenty of fresh air beneath your feet and only a rather sudden descent to follow. As a result, in poor conditions, especially of visibility, the *safest* way is to retrace steps eastwards towards Eel Crag, turn left down to Coledale Hause and then follow the path back down Gasgale Gill. In good visibility, however, AW's route down the arête forming the edge of Dove Crags gives splendid views down the crags and is a very direct way to complete the horseshoe.

For this, head north-eastwards from the summit shelter across the plateau to reach the rim of the great combe of Dove Crags and then turn left along it and follow it round, descending. There is little sign of a path down the rocks, grass and heather of the initial convex part of the descent, but then the way leads very obviously down the left bounding edge of the great hollow. The vegetated buttresses projecting into the combe are remarkably steep and very dramatic and the whole scale is much greater than could ever be imagined from the Whiteside–Hopegill Head ridge opposite. About half way down the edge, the rock-slab mentioned by AW (Grasmoor 6) is encountered and it does need

Grisedale Pike seen from the top of AW's 'Tower Ridge' on Eel Crag.

care, even when apparently dry, because there are moss patches on the gently sloping surface which tend to make it greasy; in the wet, slithering on one's bum for a few feet would prove very effective in overcoming the obstacle. It could be by-passed by traversing out left on rough ground, but this is hardly necessary.

Further down, we can confirm AW's observation that the lower lip of the hollow is definitely higher than the centre yet, most unusually, there is no large tarn here. Beyond the lip, the ground drops away quite steeply again and it will be found easier to scuttle sideways like a crab to the right over heather, grass and bilberry on a nicely cushioned descent towards the impressive ravine of Gasgale Gill. About 100ft above the beck, a narrow trod contours the slope and a left turn along this enables faster progress to be made without having to cross the stream. It passes the remains of a bield, just a single wall standing now, and then descends fairly sharply, running out onto a grassy spur which leads directly back to the car park.

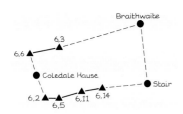

19 THE COLEDALE HORSESHOE

BEST MAP: *OS 1:25 000 Outdoor Leisure 4, North Western area*
APPROXIMATE TIME: *6½ hours*
TERRAIN: *Mostly on well-defined and firm paths but with some easy scrambling in two or three places.*

ITINERARY	Book & Fell No	Height of ascent	Distance of ascent	Cumulative distance	Height above sea level	
		feet	miles	miles	feet	mtrs
STAIR					350	107
Causey Pike	6.14	1750	1.50	1.50	2035	637
Scar Crags	6.11	320	0.75	2.25	2205	672
Sail	6.05	500	0.75	3.00	2530	773
Eel Crag	6.02	320	0.40	3.40	2749	839
COLEDALE HAUSE			1.00	4.40	2000	610
Hopegill Head	6.06	600	0.75	5.15	2525	770
Grisedale Pike	6.03	400	1.13	6.28	2593	790
BRAITHWAITE			3.00	9.28	300	91
STAIR			2.00	11.28	350	107
Totals of heights and distances of ascent		3890	11.28			

This is now a classic and justly popular circuit of some of the finest fells in the north-western part of the Lake District and must be on every fellwalker's tick-list. Once height is gained, the ridge only dips once below 2000ft (on Coledale Hause), the views are splendid and the walking exhilarating but not really strenuous. It is, however, strange (to me at least) that AW's 'Coledale Round', described in *Fellwalking with Wainwright*, omits Causey Pike and Scar Crags. This is even stranger when you consider his own advice in the Pictorial Guide (Eel Crag 6) where he illustrates and describes the walk from Stair as 'a grand ridge walk leading to Eel Crag over three intermediate tops [Causey Pike, Scar Crags and Sail], and this is the best line of ascent. The first two may be avoided (but shouldn't be).'

Because he did avoid the first two in his 'Coledale Round' and on the principle of getting the hardest part of the climbing done first, he advocated starting with the ascent of Grisedale Pike, thus giving an anti-clockwise route. On the same principle, because Causey Pike and Scar Crags are clearly included on the main ridge-line and the hardest

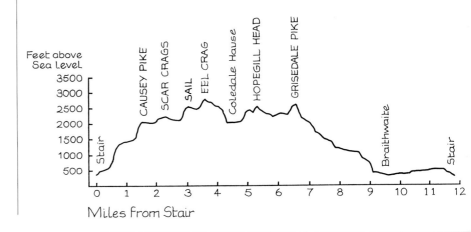

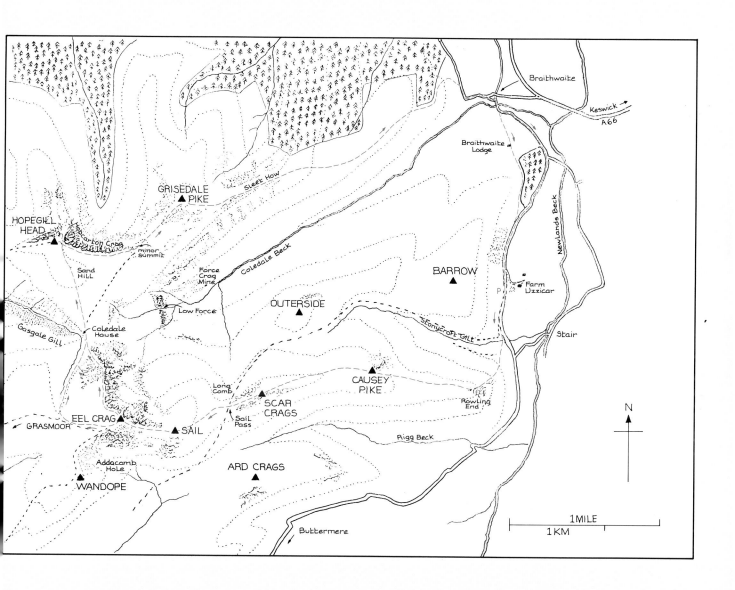

GRISEDALE PIKE ▲

HOPEGILL HEAD ▲

Hobcarton Crag

minor summit

Sand Hill

Sleet How

Braithwaite

Keswick A66

Braithwaite Lodge

Newlands Beck

Force Crag Mine

Coledale Beck

BARROW ▲

Farm Uzzicar

Low Force

OUTERSIDE ▲

Gasgale Gill

Coledale Hause

Stonycroft Gill

Stair

Long Comb

CAUSEY PIKE ▲

EEL CRAG ▲

SCAR CRAGS ▲

Rowling End

GRASMOOR

SAIL ▲

Sail Pass

Rigg Beck

N

Addacomb Hole

ARD CRAGS ▲

WANDOPE ▲

1MILE
1KM

Buttermere

ascent is the direct ascent to Causey Pike, the route I have chosen is a clockwise one. No offence intended, AW.

Beginning at Stair, or in the vicinity of the little hamlet, there is good car parking to be found on the unenclosed verge of the road (between Braithwaite and Buttermere) on the section between Farm Uzzicar and Stonycroft Gill (grid ref 233217 approximately). Ignore the old mine track leading up the north bank of Stonycroft Gill and take the signed footpath immediately south of the road bridge instead. This promptly starts to climb quite steeply, passes a bench seat (which you cannot possibly consider using yet!), turns left off a grassy path continuing up the left bank of the gill and heads directly towards the rocky nose of Rowling End rising ahead. The path zigzags up rocky ground to the right of a little crag, striding over several slanty slabs en route and is a quite sporting and attractive way to a fine viewpoint and the start of the main ridge.

The unusual and distinctive rocky knob crowning Causey Pike is now seen directly ahead and the path rises towards it through heather, then climbs up a slope of tinkling slivers of black slate until harder rock intrudes and the way steepens noticeably. The last stretch climbs the final rocky cone and involves a few easy scrambling moves, with hands on the rock, to gain the crest. AW was not certain about the altitude here and gave it as '2035′ approx', but the OS have now marked a spot height on the 1:25000 map at 637m, which is 2090ft. It *feels* every inch of that.

One very wintry day, a day of high wind, with cloud shrouding all the higher tops and with new snow plastered to the rocks, I reached the foot of the last rise and found an Irish party (their accent was unmistakable although I am sure their nationality was just a coincidence) dithering before the ascent. One of their number was clearly afraid of heights, told me so and asked my advice. This alone, under these weather conditions, was enough for me to recommend retreat, but when I saw that another was wearing trainers, a second was wearing wellies and their 'map' consisted of a piece of paper having about six numbers on it and a few handwritten names, I strongly advised it. I was glad that they accepted for I had no wish to be involved with what looked very much like an accident waiting to happen; if I had not been very familiar with the ridge myself I would have been inclined to heed my own counsel that day.

From Causey Pike the line of the ridge ahead can now be seen and the obvious path undulates over a few cairned bumps along the narrow crest for about 300 yards and then descends slightly to a depression. Beyond this it rises again and passes easily along the almost flat and grassy top edge of Scar Crags, whose rough slopes fall steeply away on the left towards Rigg Beck. There is an impressive view in the south-west towards Buttermere, down the defile between Ard Crags and Sail, and it is Sail itself which now rises ahead as the next obstacle on the ridge. A simple descent follows to the hause of Sail Pass, crossed by a path linking Braithwaite with Buttermere; on the right-hand (northern) side this traverses the head of Long Comb, the former site of a cobalt mine.

Rowling End and Causey Pike, the start of the Coledale Horseshoe.

A rather tedious pull up the eroded shoulder of Sail comes next, where several stony grooves crawl up the slope. You have to trudge up one of them, until they all coalesce into one worn path about 5ft wide as it reaches the top, which is rounded and grassy. Few walkers hesitate here; the path even by-passes the cairn on the highest point, which is in grass about 15 yards to the right and often has a deep puddle next to it. But you can clearly see the lonely head of Coledale and the old tips and remains of the Force Crag Mine, where Low Force pours over a wall of high crags. The view to Wandope across the hollow of Addacomb Hole is also worth a pause, before the much more exciting bit ahead is tackled.

A rocky descent now leads to a much narrower hause than Sail Pass and the final rise to Eel Crag (*see* page 124) beckons beyond. For the first 50ft beyond the col, the path

Looking east along Hobcarton Crag from Hopegill Head; Causey Pike and Sail in mid-distance.

wriggles up an easy rock scramble, then two easier lumps are traversed to reach a last rocky bit about 30ft high where you go easily to the left or straight up. If you go to the right and are feeling bold, you may take two or three steps along a slanting rock ramp to a splendid perch overlooking Coledale before turning back left onto the easier ground of the stony slope above and that now quickly leads to the summit of Eel Crag, the highest point on the circuit. The trig point is 100 yards to the north-west (i.e. veering right) as you emerge onto the almost flat stony top and there is a roughly constructed stone seat near to it overlooking the great sweep of crags and rocky ground that overlook Coledale.

In clear conditions it will hardly matter, but two lines of cairns will be seen leading away from the summit. One heads south-west towards Wandope and Grasmoor, the other leads along the rim of crags to the north-west. Both may be used to reach the major depression of Coledale Hause which is the key to the continuation of the circuit, but in poor conditions, especially those of snow and ice or mist, walkers unfamiliar with the top of Eel Crag are well advised to head initially to the south-west and follow the path downhill, curving rightwards (west) after about 300 yards so as to pick up and follow the course of the stream that flows north to Coledale Hause. But in clear conditions, the most direct route and the one yielding the finest views, especially back towards Sail and Causey Pike but also over the head of Coledale to Grisedale Pike, is along the rim to the north-west. When the angle begins to decline more steeply (a large cairn marks where this starts) take care in choosing your footholds as the way down is loose and stony ground running out onto scree. The normal ascent route does come this way but descent of such terrain is always more awkward than ascent and slanting rakes leading off to the left may be found more amenable than continuing close to the edge overlooking Coledale. Whichever way you reach it, arrival on the broad and grassy col of Coledale Hause always brings a release of tension.

Uphill work begins again as you head north up a slope of scree and grass towards Hopegill Head, presently hidden by the rounded top of Sand Hill, but there is now an obvious path to ease the ascent and it is simply a case of 'Switch off brain, switch on boots'. You soon curve over the top of Sand Hill and then naturally trend right a little to reach the exposed edge overlooking the shattered and vegetated Hobcarton Crag, which AW would have us believe is a haunt of dangling botanists in search of the plant *Viscaria alpina*. A last short rise leads to the delightful slaty top of Hopegill Head itself, the culminating point of three distinct ridges.

The curving ridge to the east, along the rim above Hobcarton Crag, is the one which now continues the walk, reaching a depression at the lowest point of Hobcarton Crag and then passing over a prominent minor top before descending slightly and making the final major climb of the day to Grisedale Pike. There are traces of a collapsed wall to act as a guide on this ascent but the slaty path is well worn now and leads to the exposed summit of this fine peak, the second highest on the round.

For misty conditions it is worth noting that the descent path does not continue beside the remains of the wall to the north-east but turns to the right (east) off the summit and then steeply down shaly ground, where it may not be very clear. However, once it reaches the stony crest of the Sleet How ridge it is perfectly obvious and remains so as you trundle happily back towards Braithwaite. The old direct descent to the village has been re-directed (and signed) to prevent erosion, so you will find yourself reaching the Whinlatter road just north of Braithwaite and can then turn downhill into it. Now you can either follow the road signed for Newlands and Buttermere to get back to Stair or, more pleasantly (because the road is initially narrow and walled), take the track (public footpath sign) leading to the farm of Braithwaite Lodge. A good path up the slope to the SSE brings you to the top edge of a plantation and then reaches the Buttermere road, where it is no longer walled and much less dangerous; your transport will be in sight ahead.

20 THE STONYCROFT GILL SKYLINE

BEST MAP: *OS 1:25 000 Outdoor Leisure 4, North Western area*
APPROXIMATE TIME: *3½ hours*
TERRAIN: *Mostly on good firm paths although there is some rough heathery ground and a few boggy patches.*

ITINERARY	Book & Fell No	Height of ascent	Distance of ascent	Cumulative distance	Height above sea level	
		feet	miles	miles	feet	mtrs
BRAITHWAITE					300	91
Barrow	6.23	1250	1.50	1.50	1494	455
Outerside	6.16	800	1.25	2.75	1863	568
Scar Crags	6.11	900	1.25	4.00	2205	672
Causey Pike	6.14	150	0.75	4.75	2035	637
BRAITHWAITE			3.00	7.75	300	91
Totals of heights and distances of ascent		3100	7.75			

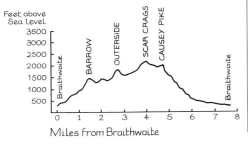

The ridge rising to Barrow and continuing over Stile End to Outerside is like an arrow fired straight into the heart of Coledale; when it ends it is overshadowed by the cirque of higher ridges which encloses it. AW did not suggest any ridge connection beyond Outerside, but it is a fairly simple matter to continue to Sail Pass and return to base along the higher ridge of Scar Crags and Causey Pike. This is clearly not a major circuit but it gives a wonderful short day and some fine views of the superbly wild scenery at the head of Coledale.

AW started from the attractive village of Braithwaite, about two miles west of Keswick, and although there is no obvious car park there are numerous small corners where a vehicle may be left. Assuming you succeed in doing this, walk out of the village centre on the Stair–Buttermere road and find the track, which is also a public footpath, leading to the farm of Braithwaite Lodge (the track leaves the road at grid ref 232235). This leads past the farm buildings, through a gate and up a field to a second gate and then trends slightly left up the slope to a finger-post beside a plantation. You are now at the foot of the ridge rising to Barrow.

Alternatively, since the walk rejoins the road near Stair, at the foot of Stonycroft Gill, you may prefer to have a bit of road walking at the beginning and a bit at the end, instead of all at once. In this case, drive out of Braithwaite on the Buttermere road and you will find numerous suitable parking places where it is unenclosed; then take the footpath slanting back along the top edge of the plantation towards Braithwaite and you will quickly reach the finger-post and the ridge.

A strip of fine turf separates bracken slopes on either side and rises invitingly straight up the crest of the ridge. Occasionally a line of pocket-steps (made where the front half of fellwalkers' boots have formed a horizontal tread in the grass slope) marks the path, but it is generally unbroken. About halfway up the ridge you reach a little notch, with a rash of mining spoil on the right side; a faint track slanting off to the left leads to the old workings of Barrow Mine. Then the bracken gives way to heather and more rock is exposed as you complete the ascent to Barrow's flat top where there are a few slaty rocks

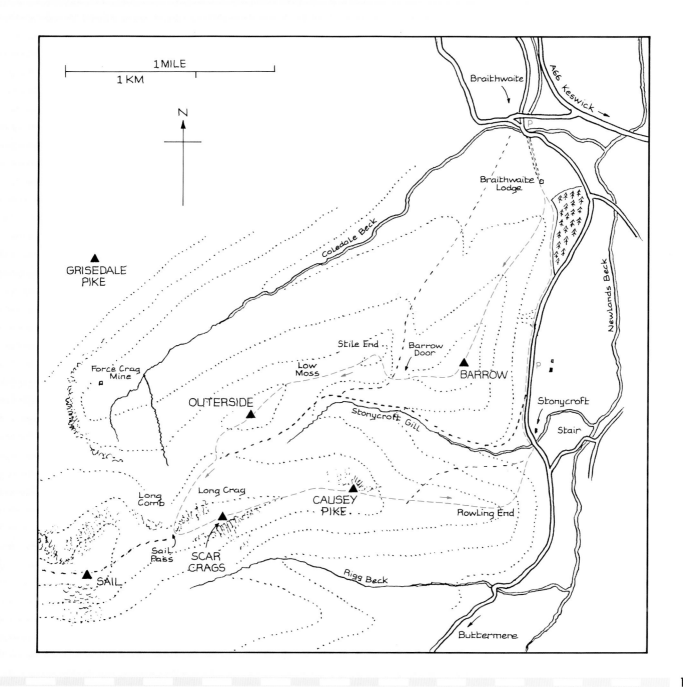

Looking south-west from Barrow: Stile End is on the right, while Outerside is sunlit. Causey Pike is shadowed top left.

and a tiny heap of stones. It is a pleasant place to linger for a moment and look to Catbells over the verdant fields of Newlands before the view is curtailed by the steep slopes rising to Rowling End and Causey Pike.

The descent is over rocky ground and then heather towards the hause of Barrow Door, which is crossed by an obvious path linking the old mine workings in Stonycroft Gill with Braithwaite. Stile End rises immediately beyond the pass, a sharp upthrust of rocks, grass and heather which is almost as high as Barrow. Walkers usually avoid it, no doubt wishing to press on by the most direct route, but Stile End clearly is a link in the ridge between Barrow and Outerside and it is worth a visit for that reason alone. There is even a faint path, found by going half-right from Barrow Door and then skirting round the steepest ground; although it soon fades on heather slopes, it is only a short climb to reach a grassier area on top with quite a good view down Coledale.

Clumps of heather and little peat groughs impede the descent to the well-named Low Moss where evil pools hide in the heather, but then firmer ground trends up towards Outerside. It looks as though the ridge will have a good rocky escarpment overlooking Coledale but the early promise soon fades and, after a short but deep trench in the heather, you soon find that peatier ground leads up the last rise. The top consists of a level ridge about 30 yards long, with a few embedded boulders at one end and a little cairn at the other, but the visual reward for this ascent is the stunning view of Sail and the rocky face of Eel Crag (*see* page 124).

To come off Outerside, a faint path continues along the edge overlooking Coledale; follow it as it veers left and down towards the head of Stonycroft Gill, crossing some juicy ground but soon turning right along a firm track. This is an old mine road and was, AW tells us (Scar Crags 2), originally intended to be a light railway supplying Lakeland's only cobalt mine which was situated in the amphitheatre of Long Comb, now looming ahead. But, as you pass the remains of a sheepfold and follow this track a little further, it soon narrows to a single shaly path and there is no sign whatever that there was ever any mining here. Thank goodness the mine failed; the mind boggles at the thought of more crumbling bricks and rusty corrugated iron-roofed buildings *here*; those of the old Force Crag Mine which can be clearly seen below at the head of Coledale are a big enough blot on the landscape.

The OS map shows a second right of way traversing across Long Comb, taking a lower level than this path, then climbing up to the top of Sail, but there is no sign of this on the ground either. The only path passes below the foot of several rock buttresses and other broken rocks (Long Crag) colonised by heather with screes falling below into Long Comb then, with a last effort, pulls up more shaly ground to reach a grassy hause where there are usually a couple of muddy puddles. This is Sail Pass where the splendid ridge to be used for the return half of the walk is joined.

Turning left (north-west), a slaty path, marked by cairns, leads up the ridge to Scar Crags, crossing several transverse peaty grooves on its almost flat top and where a careless step will leave you with a boot full of mud. If, however, you avoid these by keeping well to the right, the tremendous views down Rigg Beck come into sight. The highest point, where there is a cairn, is a little upthrust of rock overlooking a depression and the subsequent rise to Causey Pike.

Sitting here, having a sandwich and admiring the view along the steep-sided defile between Ard Crags and Sail towards Buttermere, a fellrunner (who only fifteen minutes or so earlier had run past me heading towards Sail) stopped for a chat. After mentioning that I used to particularly enjoy running over these fells myself he told me that he was training for a fellrace which would start in Buttermere, run along Ard Crags, descend towards Rigg Beck, then climb back to Causey Pike before returning along the ridges to Buttermere. He thought he would do it in something just over an hour. Looking down the ferociously steep slopes south of Scar Crags and Causey Pike, where a small oak wood clings precariously to the fellside, I did not envy him the climb back to the ridge. If he could do that round in an hour he was a lot fitter than I ever was.

Easy walking leads down to the depression, with a few more boggy trenches to cross, and the path then rises towards what looks from here like four separate little tops, with the one furthest away being Causey Pike. As you traverse them, you will pass cairns on each of the four points. Since the top of Causey Pike is made up of solid rock, with no loose stones of any size, the cairn there consists of little more than a few slaty flakes. But what a stunning place to be! It is almost like being in the crow's nest at the top of a tall ship's mast, for the ground drops away steeply on all sides except for the ridge connection. The ridges of the Newlands valley, to Robinson, to Hindscarth, to High Spy, all stand out well from here. The tiny Newlands Church can be picked out; the defile of the Sail Pass looks particularly dramatic. Looking back to Scar Crags, it resembles an upturned boat, the long narrow rock buttresses on its south flank looking like the vessel's ribs.

Descending the rocks of the summit pyramid needs care but there are several well-marked ways, clambering down for about 70 feet from ledge to ledge by slanting grooves until easier ground is reached. Then a path over flakes of black slate and well-angled embedded rocks leads down to Sleet Hause, where a cairn is built at the junction of the continuing ridge path and another leading down and across the flank of Rowling End towards Stonycroft Gill.

This latter path gives a direct return to the valley, being initially rather steep and eroded but soon becoming a much pleasanter and narrower trod traversing at a gentle angle. However, the path along the ridge above must surely be the way to complete this walk. This leads through heather to Rowling End, a mini Causey Pike, from where more intimate views over Newlands are revealed, then descends fairly steeply in zigzags to join the 'direct' route just above the pleasant little gorge of Stonycroft Gill. The road is immediately below and all that remains is to stroll back along it to your car.

The ridge to Causey Pike from Scar Crags.

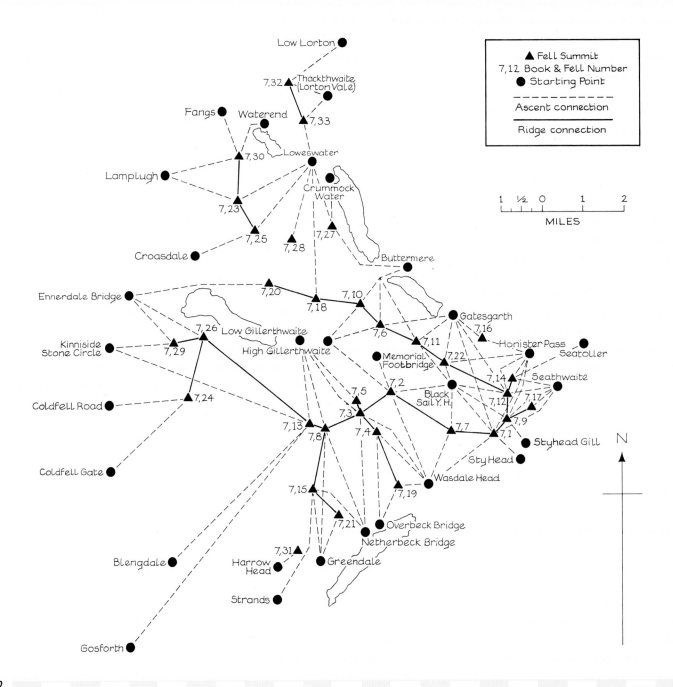

Low Lorton

7,32 Thackthwaite
(Lorton Vale)

7,33

Fangs   Waterend

7,30   Loweswater

Lamplugh

7,23

Crummock
Water

7,25

Croasdale   7,28   7,27

Buttermere

Ennerdale Bridge   7,20   7,10

7,18

Gatesgarth

7,26 Low Gillerthwaite   7,6   7,16

Kinniside   7,29   High Gillerthwaite   7,11   Honister Pass
Stone Circle   7,22   Seatoller

Memorial   7,14   Seathwaite
Footbridge   7,2   7,12   7,17

Coldfell Road   7,24   7,5   Black   7,9
Sail Y.H.   7,1

7,3   7,7   Styhead Gill
7,13   7,8   7,4   Sty Head

Coldfell Gate   Wasdale Head

7,15   7,19

Blengdale   7,21   Overbeck Bridge
Netherbeck Bridge

7,31
Harrow   Greendale
Head

Strands

Gosforth

▲ Fell Summit
7,12 Book & Fell Number
● Starting Point
------- Ascent connection
——— Ridge connection

1   ½   O   1   2

MILES

N

PART SEVEN

THE WESTERN FELLS

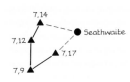

21 THE GILLERCOMB ROUND

BEST MAP: *OS 1:25 000 Outdoor Leisure 4, North Western area*
APPROXIMATE TIME: *4 hours*
TERRAIN: *Some good paths, some stony paths and some pathless rough ground.*

ITINERARY	Book & Fell No	Height of ascent	Distance of ascent	Cumulative distance	Height above sea level	
		feet	miles	miles	feet	mtrs
SEATHWAITE					450	137
Grey Knotts	7.14	1900	1.50	1.50	2287	697
Brandreth	7.12	100	0.50	2.00	2344	715
Green Gable	7.09	450	1.00	3.00	2603	801
Base Brown	7.17	130	1.00	4.00	2120	646
SEATHWAITE				1.50	5.50	450	137
Totals of heights and distances of ascent		2580	5.50			

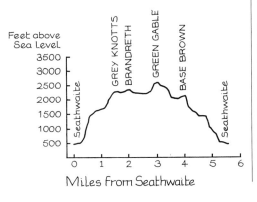

This very good but fairly short circuit is unusual because it includes both Grey Knotts and Base Brown which have been comparatively ignored, and allows discerning fellwalkers to enjoy interesting approach and descent routes away from the usual 'motorway' paths to other major fells.

Start from Seathwaite at the head of Borrowdale (grid ref 235122) where there is extensive (but rapidly filled) car parking by the roadside on the approach to the farm. An archway through farm buildings on the right of the cobbled yard is the start of the path along a walled lane to a footbridge over the infant River Derwent. Almost every other walker who crosses this bridge will now continue straight ahead on the well-used path up Sourmilk Gill, but you should turn right immediately after the bridge and cross a second footbridge, heading towards a little plantation. On the slope to the left above and beyond this, you will be able to see four or five grey spoil-tips stretching up the line of Newhouse Gill, which is the way the route goes. Just before the path reaches the plantation, you may notice a slate tablet embedded in the ground; this is a memorial to 'John Bankes Esquire 1752' which the National Trust put here 'to replace an exactly similar stone wilfully destroyed November 1887'. Human nature doesn't change much, although we keep hoping.

The path continues rather vaguely towards the famous Borrowdale Yews, which can be seen ahead, but as soon as you have crossed Newhouse Beck turn uphill beside it. The gill ahead is choked with trees and boulders but the path, the old miners' route to the plumbago mines ahead and which were the original basis of the Keswick pencil industry, swings right towards the foot of the first of the spoil-tips. It curves left before reaching it and rises towards its top, where there is a ruined building, then swings left again. On the way it passes a substantial slate slab, this time set upright, looking down to Seathwaite and backed by a sort of tumulus: another memorial to John Bankes. Sadly, vandals have been at work here also, having smashed a hole through the end of his name and obliterated the date engraved on the tablet; this must have been done since AW noted it in 1965, with its archaic spelling of 'Esquier', when it was complete.

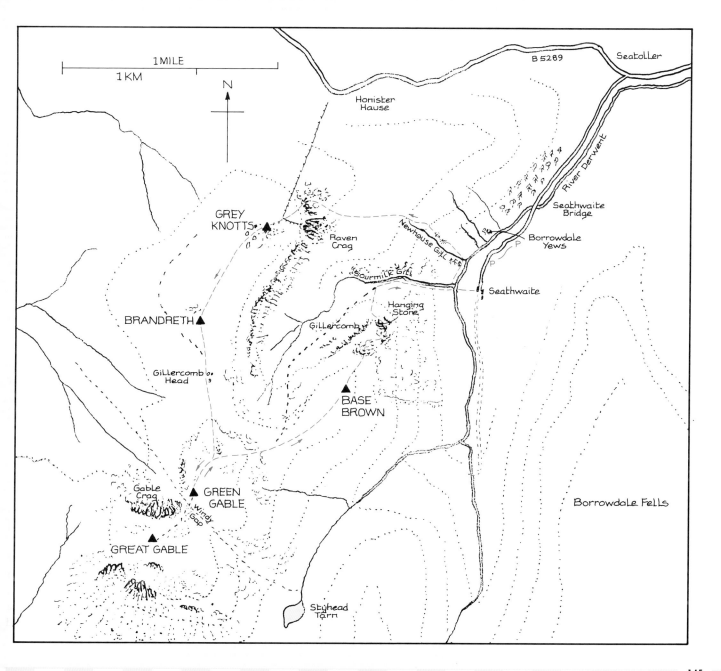

1 MILE
1 KM
N

B 5289
Seatoller

Honister
Hause

River Derwent

Seathwaite
Bridge

Newhouse Gill

Borrowdale
Yews

GREY
KNOTTS

Raven
Crag

Sourmilk Gill

P
P

Seathwaite

Hanging
Stone

BRANDRETH

Gillercomb

Gillercomb
Head

BASE
BROWN

Gable
Crag

GREEN
GABLE

Windy
Gap

Borrowdale Fells

GREAT GABLE

Styhead
Tarn

Brandreth and Raven Crag from near the head of Newhouse Gill.

The path zigzags higher, passing a second tip above which is an obvious adit and a shaft choked with holly and rowan, then climbing up the edge of another tip (more ruins) and further to the left towards the bed of the gill again, where you will find two more adits driven into the fellside immediately to the right of the watercourse. Looking at any of these shafts and adits, I cannot imagine that anyone will feel any urge to explore their innards because they are patently dangerous. Anyone who does should walk past the temptation quickly.

Just a little higher again is yet another ruin and behind it the substantial intake wall. Crossing this obviously caused AW a few problems but there is now a solid ladder-stile to make it easy to complete the ascent past a final few ruins and excavations and onto open moor. You have gained about 1000ft in height, are above the lip of the hanging valley of Gillercomb and now have a fine view of Raven Crag (known to rock-climbers as Gillercomb Buttress) which overlooks it, with Green Gable in sight beyond. The path promptly disappears but easy slopes now stretch towards Grey Knotts. The steep and in places overhanging walls of Raven Crag are clearly to be avoided but by trending towards the right-hand skyline, well to the right of Raven Crag, grassy rakes between little rock walls enable easy progress to be made upwards, with no one obvious route. When you meet a wire fence, simply follow it uphill: you will reach a corner where two fences join at a stile and can then cross to join a good path and complete the ascent to the south-west, past two old fence posts, to find the summit cairn just past a third, on top of a rock outcrop directly above it. This cairn is on the east top, in an area of splendidly rough rocks and with good views to Pillar and the High Stile ridge, although these are seen even better from the cairned west top about 200 yards away.

The old fence line, whose iron posts led the way up the last bit of the ascent to the east (main) top of Grey Knotts, now runs along a depression between the two tops to the south-west, passing several attractive tarns trapped in the rocks and continuing over stony ground, with little gain in height, along the broad top of the ridge for half a mile to reach Brandreth, whose large summit cairn has an iron boundary post stuck in it. Despite the continuing grand views to the north-west, the prospect due south towards Green Gable and Great Gable now steals all the attention. The old fence posts continue down more stony ground to pass three tarns on the hause of Gillercomb Head, where the 'motorway' path joins from Honister, then a cairned path rises for a mile, firstly over rough ground and then shale, on the climb to Green Gable.

You will probably reach the top with some relief, but it is a wonderful place to halt anyway. On a fine day, you are unlikely to be alone here but you cannot possibly resent sharing such a superb situation with others. Gable Crag, the tremendous Ennerdale face of Great Gable, is now seen in detail, the Scafell massif is seen to the south, and the Buttermere fells and High Stile ridge to the north-west. Great Gable itself looks over-poweringly close to its smaller and not-so-green neighbour and many walkers will under-standably feel that they must go the rest of the way to its top. It is, however, a further half-mile and 500ft of ascent and the climb beyond Windy Gap is seen by many walkers as rather intimidating, especially under winter conditions, as there are some awkwardly angled slabs and plenty of loose stones to contend with. Don't forget that you have to return the same way. For these reasons, but also because AW's ridge-line goes from Green Gable, not Great, to Base Brown, the extra distance and height is excluded from the tables at the beginning of this chapter.

Therefore, reverse the last part of the ascent from Green Gable towards Brandreth for about a quarter of a mile to a large boulder outcrop. Just before arrival there, a line of cairns marks a path leading off down a broad ridge north-east towards Base Brown. A stony descent runs out onto a grassy hause where there is a National Trust 'footpath' sign pointing down into Gillercomb. Ignoring this (unless overtaken by mist when it will be a good escape route), continue up the grassy slope of the ridge beyond to reach the fine rocky top of Base Brown. The view to Glaramara and the Scafells are worth enjoying but I fear few people linger here.

The continuation of the ridge descends now in two long but distinct steps: down grass to a few rocks marking the end of the first step, then down more grass to where the easy progress is halted by an upsurge of rocks forming the second step. As soon as this is reached look for a narrow path going right and marked by some very light-coloured (almost white) rocks and slabs. This leads to the top of an obvious, wide and vegetated gully which splits the rim of crags overlooking Gillercomb and, although easy at the top, it is very awkward at the bottom. Therefore, unless you are prepared to leave bits of your breeches or skin sticking to the greasy rocks, it is best ignored. Much better to cross the head of this gully, still going right, and the path will then be seen below, apparently descending towards Seathwaite. In fact as you lose height the path then cuts back left, directly below Hanging Stone. This is a big block with a flat base which is balanced with apparently more than half its weight overhanging a fine compact crag. It is about 50ft directly above the path, but I don't think there's much chance that a loud cough will bring it down just yet. As you continue traversing beyond it, it becomes obvious that there is plenty of rock above to hold it securely in place. The path leads to the foot of the rough gully mentioned above and then fades in grass and boulders, but the downward continuation of the gully is easy-angled and grassy and it leads pleasantly to a junction with the main Seathwaite–Brandreth path just before it drops over the lip of Gillercomb.

From here the reconstructed path passes close to the upper waterfall of Sourmilk Gill where it spouts over a small crag, then passes through a gate in the intake wall and scrambles easily down some well-scratched rocky grooves beneath trees to where the second falls begin. As the waters slide down a long narrow groove into a basin and then foam down slabs, the path curves round to their foot and finally reaches the bottom of the gill. It is an attractive finish to the day, for all that remains is to cross a ladder-stile and the footbridge back to Seathwaite. The finish will be even better if you remember that the excellent little café here can almost always be relied on for tea and scones.

Grey Knotts seen from the slope below Green Gable;
Dale Head and High Spy in mid-distance; Skiddaw on
the skyline.

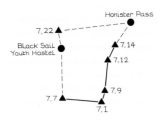

22 THE HEAD OF ENNERDALE

BEST MAP: OS 1:25 000 Outdoor Leisure 4, North Western area
APPROXIMATE TIME: 7 hours
TERRAIN: Generally good paths, although most are over rough ground.

ITINERARY	Book & Fell No	Height of ascent	Distance of ascent	Cumulative distance	Height above sea level	
		feet	miles	miles	feet	mtrs
HONISTER PASS					1150	351
Haystacks	7.22	1050	2.25	2.25	1900	582
BLACK SAIL YH			1.25	3.50	1000	305
Kirk Fell	7.07	1700	1.50	5.00	2630	802
Great Gable	7.01	990	1.33	6.33	2949	899
Green Gable	7.09	150	0.50	6.83	2603	801
Brandreth	7.12	200	1.00	7.83	2344	715
Grey Knotts	7.14	50	0.50	8.33	2287	697
HONISTER PASS			1.00	9.33	1150	351
Totals of heights and distances of ascent		4140	9.33			

As mentioned in the Introduction, although the ridge-line map based on the tops that AW linked shows a circuit enclosing the whole of Ennerdale (used by the Ennerdale Fell Race), this round will take an average walker 13–15 hours, thus becoming an endurance test rather than an enjoyable walk. The walk described here, covering the fells at the head of Ennerdale is, I feel, a much more reasonable proposition and, at the same time, is indeed a high mountain round of exceptional quality and wonderful views.

Start from the car park on Honister Hause (grid ref 225135), but don't expect to find space there if you can't get out of bed promptly in the morning. From here a stony track, signed by a finger-post 'Great Gable, Dubs', rises beyond the slate-dressing floor and buildings used by the old quarries and climbs to the west. Sections of the track have been much improved recently but a few traces of wooden sleepers still remain from when this incline was used for transporting quarried slate. At the top of the rise, where the track

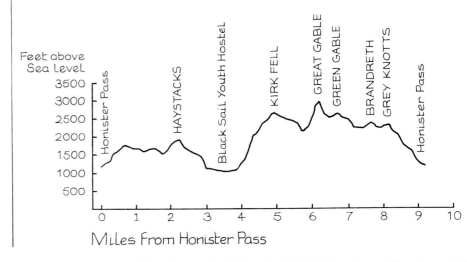

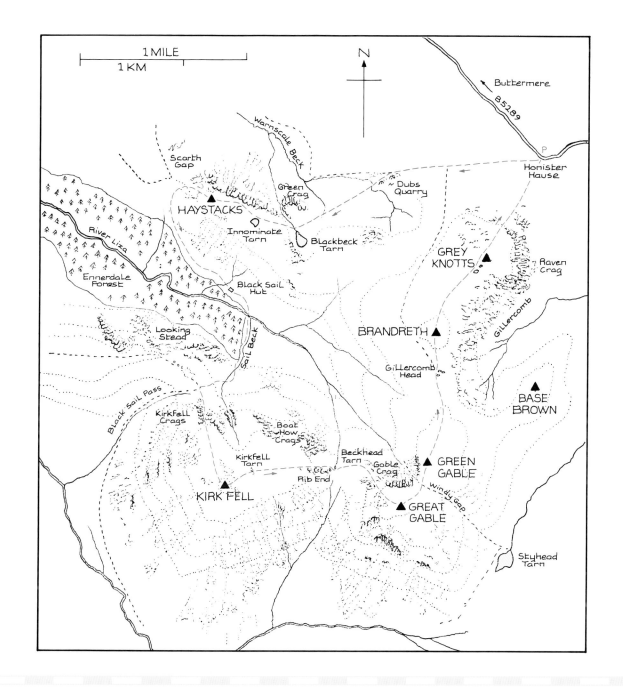

runs along a little embankment, an obvious cairned path turns left (south) towards Brandreth, but keep straight ahead, for Haystacks – AW's favourite fell – is the first objective. As you descend slightly towards the old Dubs slate quarries, this 'shaggy terrier in the company of foxhounds' comes almost fully into view, its sides riven by dank gullies and with Pillar peering over its dishevelled shoulders. Pass the old quarry hut (I was pleased to find that it has been re-roofed and virtually rebuilt) and then descend beside some old slate tips to cross Warnscale Beck on stepping-stones.

A newly pitched and obvious path now leads south-west up the eroded slope beyond, trends to the right of a fine lump of rock, crosses rockier ground above the unseen Green Crag and reaches a defile where a stream drains the tear-shaped Blackbeck Tarn. Buttermere comes into view from here. Across the beck, the path swings right and climbs to a higher level, disclosing the beautiful Innominate Tarn (where AW's ashes are scattered), then rises steadily to the WNW and over a little rock barrier of easy-angled slabs to reach the short and almost level summit ridge. Surprisingly, there is a little tarn in a trough immediately behind it and two iron posts and two cairns, one at each end, so you may argue which is the highest point while you admire a fine view to High Crag to the north-west and consider the descent to Scarth Gap.

AW's advice to a novice lost in mist on Haystacks was that he 'should kneel down and pray for safe deliverance', which is a fair comment on the complexity of this fascinating fell. However, anyone who definitely makes it to the top next to the tarn in mist, should head for another iron post on the west side of the tarn. Then the path follows an easy rock groove towards another post and continues to reach a prominent cairn marking the next stage of the descent down more steep ground to a little lip and another tiny tarn. From here several paths lead down rough ground and scree and it is a toss-up which you choose, but all reach the hause of Scarth Gap where you turn down-hill to the south-west and follow the track beside the forest fence towards Ennerdale.

The path soon leads up the valley past the Black Sail Hut, which has been a Youth Hostel for as long as I can remember (it is over forty years since I carried my tent and a huge weight of other gear from Langdale via Bowfell, Scafell Pike and Great Gable to camp near here) and then a morass has to be crossed on boulders to a footbridge over the River Liza. The next stretch is of course uphill, very evidently so as the path can be seen climbing fairly close to the edge of Sail Beck, passing a couple of attractive cascades. Higher up, although a fainter trod traverses to the left below Boat How Crags, the path needed swings away onto the slope on the right to avoid a very deep ravine, then completes the ascent to the hause. It is a stiff pull and I was glad of the excuse to pause, chat with and congratulate four lads cutting new drainage channels and carrying out other reconstruction work on the path up here, funded by the National Trust. As well as other shorter ones in the area, they had also worked on the excellent new route up Brown Tongue to Scafell.

A line of iron fence posts runs across the hause, pointing the way to the north-west to Looking Stead and Pillar, but on the south-eastern side, towards Kirk Fell, which is where we pick up the ridge-line again, the steep rocks of Kirkfell Crags appear to present an impregnable obstacle to walkers. It comes as no surprise therefore that a path of reddish-coloured stones curves left below the steepest rock buttress to avoid it and this is also the obvious way to start the ascent. Going up this path, however, you are soon faced by three steep gullies, the central one of which has a great deal of red scree in it. These all look pretty horrible and, although some walkers do thrutch and scrabble up them, it is advisable to cut back to the right, just before reaching the foot of these gullies, where a short rake quickly leads out onto the nose of the ridge above the steepest buttress and you will spot another iron fence post. Here you join a delightful path, twisting and climbing up little rock steps past more fence posts (or their sockets cut in the rock even when the posts are missing) and this leads to two cairns close together at the top of the rise. It is a good spot to rest for a while and maybe have a bite of lunch.

Kirk Fell (centre) and Pillar, with Ennerdale on right, seen from Green Gable.

It is half a mile SSE from here to the top of Kirk Fell, which is as yet unseen, although the distinctive shape of Great Gable, looking from here like a volcanic plug, stands out boldly to the ESE and may falsely tempt you to go that way. Do not desert the fence posts: they continue to steer you over mossy and grassy ground on this sloping plateau, then across rashes of boulders and past more outcrops as the top comes nearer. The highest fence post is, appropriately, stuck into the rocks forming the circular windbreak on the highest point of the fell so there is absolutely no excuse for not finding it. The view is unquestionably dominated by Great Gable but there are fine views to Grasmoor and to High Stile, and you may even see the little tarn on top of Haystacks.

Stony ground now leads towards Great Gable and you pick up a path that follows more fence posts and sneaks between the two little tarns that collectively constitute Kirkfell Tarn. This takes you to where a rocky descent has to be made down Rib End towards Beckhead Tarn which lies, with another little tarn, on the hause between Kirk Fell and Great Gable. Beyond that, the approach to Great Gable is obviously up a sharp spur, the mountain's north-west ridge, which is in full view from here; obvious, that is, until it ends in a band of much steeper rocks. In fact, the easy-angled ridge is very straight-forward, but then a wearisome struggle follows, scrabbling up, over or round big, sharp-edged boulders that litter the upper slopes. It is a relief to reach easier ground at last and make your way over to the final rocky upthrust and the summit cairn. Pause here for a moment before the Fell and Rock Memorial plaque on a north-facing rock; amongst the seventeen names engraved there are those of Herford, Oppenheimer and Jeffcoat, familiar to all Lake District rock-climbers who still hold to the great traditions of adventure-climbing that they, with others, pioneered. The views from the top are all around the compass, but the finest is that from the Westmorland Cairn, overlooking Wasdale, found by walking 100 yards south-west of the summit to the very edge of the south-face crags.

Well-scratched rocks and a line of cairns lead from Great Gable's summit to the north and then curve right before reaching the great precipices of Gable Crag facing down Ennerdale, then a stony path skitters down a groove or gully which has too much loose rubble and awkwardly angled slabs for complete comfort even under good conditions. But the final bit of the descent to Windy Gap is simple and the short rise up the far slope to Green Gable is easier still. Gable Crag is a stunning sight from here, as are the views down Ennerdale and to the Scafells, probably better than from the top of Great Gable itself.

More old fence posts now show the line of the long descent, if the bootmarks of thousands of predecessors fail to make it obvious, to the north, as far as the three peat-rimmed tarns on Gillercomb Head where there is an incongruous iron gate in the middle of a non-existent fence. From here the most obvious path, which is cairned, swings away to the north-east, goes over a shoulder of Brandreth and by-passes Grey Knotts entirely, but the true ridge-line, and our route, follows more occasional fence posts up the rough slope northwards and climbs gently to the stony top of Brandreth, the fifth top of the day but one of small distinction compared to those already visited. An undulating descent over more rough ground along the broad line of the continuing ridge to the north-east, and following a sometimes less than obvious path, soon leads past a few more tarns. These are on the edge of some particularly rocky ground and the summit cairn of Grey Knotts will be spotted on top of a rock outcrop to the right of and above the line of the path.

All that remains to complete the circuit is to return to Honister Hause and for this you need to turn east down a grassy groove beside the summit outcrop on Grey Knotts, marked by two more fence posts. The path quickly leads to a point where two intact fences form a corner and a rough path steers downhill to the north-east beside one of them. Before long, the disused buildings on the hause come into sight below and although the path remains unrelentingly steep, a nicely constructed section near the end makes the finish easier than you might have expected, a happy end to a superb round.

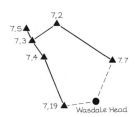

23 THE MOSEDALE SKYLINE

BEST MAP: *At OS 1:25 000 scale, both Outdoor Leisure 6, South Western area and Outdoor Leisure 4, North Western area are needed. On a single map, the whole walk will be found on OS Landranger 89, West Cumbria.*

APPROXIMATE TIME: *7 hours*

TERRAIN: *Often on reasonable paths but over ground which is a good mixture of grass, rock and scree; anybody wearing high heels or casual shoes would be well advised to go no further than the bar of the Wasdale Head Inn.*

ITINERARY	Book & Fell No	Height of ascent	Distance of ascent	Cumulative distance	Height above sea level	
		feet	miles	miles	feet	mtrs
WASDALE HEAD					250	76
Kirk Fell	7.07	2330	1.25	1.25	2630	802
Pillar	7.02	1150	2.50	3.75	2927	892
Scoat Fell	7.03	300	1.25	5.00	2760	841
Steeple	7.05	70	0.25	5.25	2687	819
Scoat Fell	7.03	140	0.25	5.50	2760	841
Red Pike (Wasdale)	7.04	210	0.75	6.25	2707	826
Yewbarrow	7.19	680	1.75	8.00	2058	628
WASDALE HEAD			2.50	10.50	250	76
Totals of heights and distances of ascent		4880	10.50			

The Mosedale Horseshoe has generally been considered to start by going up the Black Sail Pass and then on to Pillar, but this is a cop-out, for Kirk Fell is clearly part of the skyline. It is also quite clear from Peter Linney's ridge-line map based on the Pictorial Guide that Kirk Fell *must* be included; indeed a case could be made for including Great Gable as well; but let us be *reasonable* and forget Great Gable this time, for the circuit described here is as good a day's fellwalking as you will get anywhere. However, although the specifications show the ridge-line between Kirk Fell and Pillar, I shall also mention the excellent alternative of the High Level Route.

The start is from Wasdale Head (grid ref 186088) and there is parking space on the

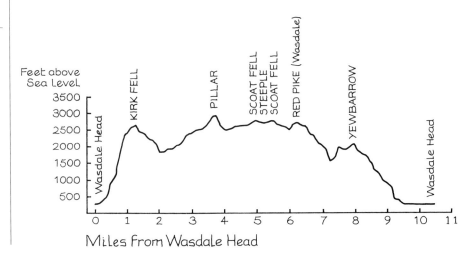

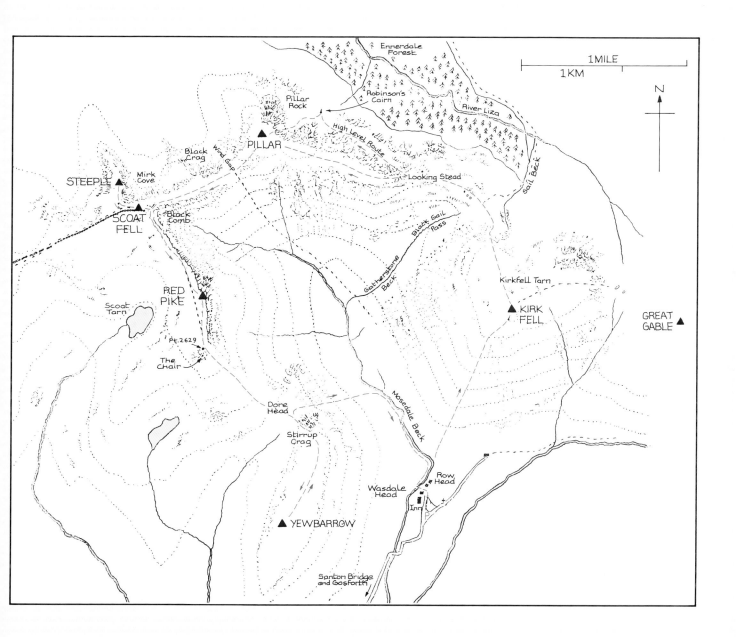

green, a triangle of enclosed land about 100 yards before the tarmac ends at the Wasdale Head Inn, or on the public car park in front of it (which will leave you much more strategically placed for a jar of throat lubrication later). From this latter point, take the bridleway signed for Black Sail Pass, turning right (north-east) beside the Mosedale Beck. Do not cross the shapely packhorse bridge immediately ahead (you will on the way back) but keep the beck on your left and follow the track past the farm buildings at Row Head, rising gently up to a gate in the intake wall. The bridleway for Black Sail Pass turns left here, as will any walker who wishes to avoid Kirk Fell, but you take a few deep breaths and start going uphill in a straight line, up the SSW ridge of Kirk Fell.

AW had a lot of fun exaggerating the description of this ascent. He portrayed it (Kirk Fell 4) as 'a relentless and unremitting treadmill, a turf-clutching crawl.... Back buttons cannot stand the strain, and wearers of braces are well advised to profit from a sad experience of the author on this climb and take a belt as reserve support.' His drawing shows a fellwalker toiling up a 45-degree slope, and it if truly were 45 degrees then few would ever bother. The fact is, however, that the angle is about 30 degrees, and I have measured height and distance (from the intake wall, not the pub) and used my protractor to do the calculation, quite apart from walking up Mosedale to take a sideways look at it. It is all a question of *attitude*. The ridge does look diabolically steep when you see it head on. It looks infernally bare and open. It looks as though, if you slipped on it half way up, you would trundle all the way down to the bottom at an ever increasing speed and with nothing to stop you. But look positively at the problem and you will realise that all you have to do is to walk uphill steadily at what any reasonable fellwalker can only honestly describe as a reasonable angle, on a fair path (because there is one there now) and you will have a direct, albeit a super-direct, route straight to the top of Kirk Fell. I will admit that it would be trying in high wind, but so will many other places in Lakeland. Have courage and get stuck in! And do not let *our* ridge diagram put you off either; ours looks even worse than AW's drawing.

Although there are two tops on Kirk Fell, there is only one which concerns us, and this higher one is marked by a stone windbreak with an iron fence post stuck in it. Walkers who have braved the SSW ridge may feel that AW's ethereal presence will smile benignly on them if they rest here, so long as they do not stay for too long, of course.

Iron posts lead across the broad and sloping summit plateau and mark the way over occasionally mossy and sometimes stony ground, leaving behind the views of Great Gable that dominated the scene from the summit and heading towards the great bulk of Pillar to the north-west. It is easy going downhill and as the rocks of Kirkfell Crags draw closer, a path materialises, still shadowing the posts, and leads to cairns at the top of the downfall overlooking the Black Sail Pass. This path continues down a series of little rock steps and ledges and even when the fence posts disappear you can still see the slots in the rock where they used to be. There is one awkward place on the top of the main buttress, but a helpful ramp leads to the right and down to a shaly path on easy ground, curving left to reach the top of the pass.

You did not lose a lot of height on the descent from the top of Kirk Fell and should be feeling quite fresh to take the rising path which strides easily along the ridge towards Pillar. Initially this sticks close to the line of the fence posts but, after passing a couple of little tarns, it trends left to skirt round the shoulder of Looking Stead. The posts, however, lead up to a cairn on its top and it is worth making this slight diversion and ascent for a good view not only of Ennerdale but also of Pillar's dramatic northern slopes. In particular, it is a good place from which to pick out the path of the High Level Route traversing the fellside to Pillar Rock which must be mentioned as, unusually, it gives a more interesting way to Pillar than the ridge route. I will return to it at the end of this chapter.

From Looking Stead a short descent leads to a depression, where the path is rejoined, and this now zigzags quite steeply up the rough ground of the ridge, although it soon trends left and away from the edge on the right. Many of the posts have disappeared on this steep section but some soon reappear intermittently and follow the edge faithfully, even when the path cuts corners, thus giving a reliable guide even in almost white-out conditions. After two further steeper sections, which are rockier rather than grassy, you walk onto the broad, domed top of Pillar mountain, where it seems that most of the available stones have been used to build a cairn, a couple of windbreaks and the trig point. There is no resemblance to a 'pillar' of any kind and it is only when you stroll fifty yards to the north and look down the slope that the top of Pillar Rock comes into view and it is then clear how the Rock gave its name to the mountain.

Now you may prance about or stroll around up here as you will, but when the urge to get a move on seizes you again, follow the line of cairns heading south-west and you will find yourself descending steeply towards Wind Gap. You will need to be more careful now: it is easy enough, but the erosion of boots and weather has left rough slabs exposed at awkward angles, with slithery grit underfoot, and it will be a relief to reach the col. Like Windy Gap between Great and Green Gable, this one, Wind Gap, is well-named and funnels the prevailing sou'westerlies most effectively. An obvious path now leads up the slope beyond, where you will have an entertaining tussle with some huge boulders until you can land safely on a level grassy stretch on the top of Black Crag. There is some splendid rock scenery here, but you will appreciate it better from Scoat Fell which lies ahead, beyond a further very slight depression. Once again the path struggles over more chaotically piled boulders to reach the end of a wall, above. This wall is the Ennerdale Fence, running westwards for miles and it crosses the highest point on Scoat Fell only 50 paces west of here, so it is no accident that a cairn is piled on top of the wall to mark the summit. (The OS is rather confusing here, naming three Scoat Fells; the highest point is at grid ref 160113, which the OS name as 'Little Scoat Fell'.)

The east face of Pillar Rock seen from Robinson's Cairn.

Looking across Mirk Cove to Pillar from Scoat Fell.

Walking west beside the wall you will be looking across part of Mirk Cove to what is unmistakably Steeple and in about 150 paces will reach a large cairn marking where a narrow and delightful path trips down to a slender neck of land and then climbs easily to Steeple's top. I think that the view across Mirk Cove to the arête and rock faces of Black Crag and to Pillar is quite one of the finest in these western fells; I can sit here for half an hour, and often have done, watching the shadows chase each other across that wonderful landscape.

With Red Pike as the next top on the horseshoe you must return to the wall-end on Scoat Fell (just past the highest point) and once again pick your way down those piled boulders – but only until you reach grass and easy ground again, when a narrow grooved path cuts sharply back right and curves around the rim of Black Comb, heading SSE and soon gently climbing the edge of the fine escarpment leading to Red Pike. Stay on the edge, not only for the fine cliff scenery and grand views on the left down Mosedale to Kirk Fell, but because the main path cuts across the slope a little lower down and by-passes both a viewpoint cairn and the summit cairn. Unlike the cairns on Pillar, you certainly could not prance around this one, for it is perched precariously on the edge of space, with a terrific drop falling away below your feet; only a real prat would fool around here.

Now you are here, you will begin to grasp that all the uphill work has been done (unless you are a complete purist, see later) for a pleasant path now leads gently southwards and downhill along the rest of the rim. In about 600 paces, just before it reaches a prominent cairn in a rash of boulders (AW's Point 2629, OS spot height 801m), it turns downhill and gallops off towards Dore Head. But just south of this cairn, only 100 paces over rocky ground, is The Chair. This is built from substantial slabs of stone and has been there a lot longer than any of us has been alive. It is worth a visit and you don't want any know-all looking scornfully at you when you say you've traversed Red Pike *but failed to visit The Chair*, do you? Having done that, you may return and pick up the path again and follow it fairly easily (although there is some rough ground on the last stretch) to Dore Head.

This is where purists will not hesitate, for AW's blessed ridge-line continues to Yewbarrow (and our route details, heights gained etc, include this). They might be put off a bit by the sight of the path heading for the steep rocks of Stirrup Crag (which defend Yewbarrow above Dore Head) and particularly by the upper belt of crags, but generations of fellwalkers have struggled successfully up there with rucksacks and dogs and walking sticks (sometimes with all three) and so far as I know nobody has ever fallen off. It is about 450ft of ascent from Dore Head to the cairn on top of Stirrup Crag and in the next half-mile, assuming you are a purist, you (not me, because I've been there many times and am only going to accompany you in spirit) will gain a further 40ft of altitude and finally be able to touch the summit cairn. Then you can retrace your steps to return to

Dore Head, reversing the route of ascent, with some bum-slithering and careful footwork. You will do a mile and 500ft more of ascent than me today and can feel superior.

The descent from Dore Head to Mosedale Beck used to be a good scree run, but the scree is all in piles at the bottom of the slope now and, as you will see, what is left is pretty nasty: exposed earth and rocks. *Do not even think of it.* Instead, *carefully* pick a line down the grass slopes to the left of the old scree run and you will soon find yourself swinging right and on the obvious path leading back to Wasdale Head.

I promised to return to the High Level Route as a splendid way to Pillar; a way superior, for once, to the ridge route.

Leaving Looking Stead, the iron fence posts lead down to a slight depression, start to climb the slope beyond towards steeper rocky ground and then appear to end. About 50 yards beyond the last post, and above it on the right, a cairn on a little rock bluff marks the start of the High Level Route, the path being below it and starting with a short descent. It then traverses across the slope, below crags above and above crags below; it is fairly sensational and certainly spectacular but without any difficulty. It runs out onto a broad and bouldery rake which rises to Robinson's Cairn, a splendid and unmistakable memorial to John Wilson Robinson, a great cragsman and walker who ascended Pillar Rock over a hundred times. The tremendous east face of Pillar Rock now rises before you, with the Shamrock (= Sham Rock) to its left, separated by a deep gully. The walker's route to Pillar *mountain*, not to the Pillar Rock (which needs rock-climbing or high-grade scrambling ability), now becomes clearer also as it is well-used. The path descends slightly from the cairn to cross a stony hollow, then turns left up a low rock ridge and up scree to reach the start of the Shamrock Traverse. This is an obvious wide ledge or rake slanting bottom left to top right above the Shamrock, which often has loose stones on it but is not dangerous so long as it is traversed carefully. When the rake ends, continue on a rising traverse and follow the path as it turns quite steeply up the slope and finishes up loose scree, emerging onto the summit plateau of Pillar.

The rock scenery en route is superb but, when moving, keep your eyes on where you are placing your feet. You will pass by the top of Walker's Gully; this is named not after any walker, but after a chap named Walker who carelessly fell down it to the bottom of Pillar Rock, with fatal results. So make sure that once you have started on the Shamrock Traverse you only follow the path going upwards thereafter. Any other 'paths' here are strictly for rock-climbers.

Looking back from Point 2629 to Red Pike's main top (left) and Pillar.

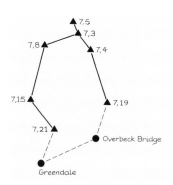

24 THE NETHER BECK RIM

BEST MAP: *At 1:25 000 scale, both OS Outdoor Leisure 6, South Western area and Outdoor Leisure 4, North Western area are needed, although almost all the walk is on Sheet 6. On a single map the whole walk will be found on either Harvey's Mountain Map 'Scafell' (1:40 000) or OS Landranger 89, West Cumbria (1:50 000).*
APPROXIMATE TIME: *7–8 hours*
TERRAIN: *A mixture of steep grassy slopes, rocky ground and a short scramble. Paths are very faint between Middle Fell and Haycock.*

ITINERARY	Book & Fell No	Height of ascent	Distance of ascent	Cumulative distance	Height above sea level	
		feet	miles	miles	feet	mtrs
OVERBECK BRIDGE					250	76
GREENDALE		0	2.00	2.00	250	76
Middle Fell	7.21	1650	1.50	3.50	1908	582
Seatallan	7.15	750	1.50	5.00	2266	692
Haycock	7.08	1050	2.00	7.00	2618	797
Scoat Fell	7.03	450	1.00	8.00	2760	841
Steeple	7.05	70	0.25	8.25	2687	819
Scoat Fell	7.03	140	0.25	8.50	2760	841
Red Pike (Wasdale)	7.04	210	0.75	9.25	2707	826
Yewbarrow	7.19	680	1.75	11.00	2058	628
OVERBECK BRIDGE			1.50	12.50	250	76
Totals of heights and distances of ascent		5000	12.50			

This is a superb high mountain round only marred by about 1½ miles of road linking the two arms of the circuit – a small price to pay for such a splendid day's fellwalking.

It you can arrange motor transport between Overbeck Bridge and Greendale you have no problem at all; if you have only got Shanks' Pony I suggest it is better to get the bit of road-walking done first and start from the National Trust car park at Overbeck Bridge, grid ref 168068, to which you will descend at the end of the day – and don't forget your voluntary contribution in the box – then head south-west beside Wastwater. You soon reach Netherbeck Bridge and then the road switchbacks below the steep slopes of Middle Fell, defended by numerous crags and outcrops, before you turn right at the first junction and continue as far as Greendale. From here a wide green track closely shadows the beck dancing below the great buttresses of Buckbarrow and gives about 400ft of ascent until it forks, as the gorge begins to narrow. Here you need to swing right

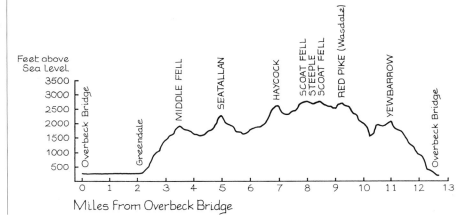

Miles from Overbeck Bridge

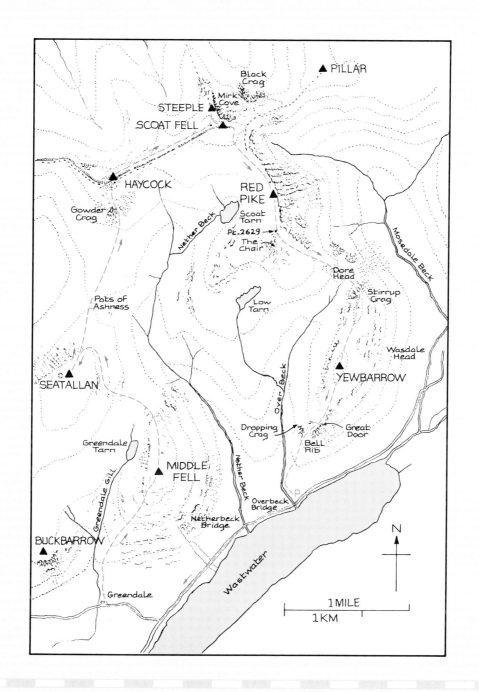

▲ PILLAR

Black Crag

Mirk Cove

STEEPLE

SCOAT FELL

HAYCOCK

Gowder Crag

RED PIKE

Scoat Tarn

Pt. 2629

The Chair

Nether Beck

Mosedale Beck

Dore Head

Stirrup Crag

Pots of Ashness

Low Tarn

Over Beck

Wasdale Head

SEATALLAN

YEWBARROW

Greendale Tarn

Dropping Crag

Great Door

Bell Rib

MIDDLE FELL

Greendale Gill

Nether Beck

Overbeck Bridge

P

Netherbeck Bridge

BUCKBARROW

N

Wastwater

1 MILE

1 KM

Greendale

(north-east) up another grass slope and then follow cairns over a stony section and up the broad ridge beyond. The path is narrow and occasionally unclear but it leads to a fine tilted rock slab and a large cairn of pinky-grey rock on top of the highest outcrop just above it. Here you are on Middle Fell, and able to survey the whole of the rest of the day's round except Steeple, which is just hidden behind Scoat Fell. Interestingly, Scafell looks higher than Scafell Pike from here.

Seatallan is the next top, seen to the north-west over Greendale Gill.

Fifty paces left (west) of the summit cairn, the ground drops steeply towards Greendale Tarn but there is a grassy path along the top edge which then turns down between outcrops towards the broad hause linking Middle Fell to Seatallan. The hause is progressively soggy and then sopping wet and you will be glad you greased your boots, but as you mince delicately across you will spot a grassy path rising up the slope opposite. Unfortunately, it is one of those paths that looks obvious from a distance and then vanishes as you get close, so when you lose this one, as you surely will, just continue uphill, slanting rightwards onto a sloping grass shelf below a rash of scree and boulders.

As I toiled up here with my two shadows, Henry and Freddie, some sheep on the skyline above watched disdainfully and I swear that a couple of ravens were eyeing up Freddie, the smaller dog, and wondering if he would make a meal. When I reached a cairn on a shoulder I could at last turn up the ridge to Seatallan. There is no path but it is a straightforward climb up grass, and the sheep now scattered in all directions, realising that I was not quite so moribund as they thought after all. A large cairn appeared ahead, but just 100 yards beyond it is a trig point (S 5762) which is normally found on the highest point of a fell. Just west of that is a huge mound of stones, now scooped out to form a windbreak, although they are apparently part of an ancient tumulus. It seemed to me that the cairn, not the trig point or the tumulus, is on the highest point.

Descend the slope to the north, reversing most of the last part of the ascent, and head towards Haycock on a faint path which is just visible where it runs across a different kind of grass on the hause, near the little pools known as Pots of Ashness. Youngsters who have only ever seen hay in bales, or those Swiss rolls, may wonder what a haycock is, or was but, as the grasslands below it are traversed, the shape of the fell ahead will give a good idea. The rocks of Gowder Crag project from the middle of the slope ahead and look insignificant until you have traversed another juicy stretch of ground when you realise that they present a real obstacle. AW suggested going well left of the rocks but the screes there do not look attractive and I found it quite easy and pleasant to go up the right edge of Gowder Crag where it was steep but grassy. Beyond the crag and having gained useful height, the choice is clear: scree, or scree. You must, therefore, toil up it for a short distance until it runs out onto an easier-angled grassier fellside, reaching a cairn built on a prominent rock outcrop. About 300 yards north of this, on the stony cap of

Steeple seen from the rim of Mirk Cove.

Haycock, is a large cairn on the south side of the substantial wall which traverses the top of the fell. On the north side a second cairn has been hollowed out to form a tear-shaped windbreak. The most interesting view is undoubtedly the one across the depression to the north-east, to Scoat Fell and Steeple, which is where we now go.

The way is obvious and is marked by the wall; the stony ground is soon left behind and easy walking on close-cropped turf follows, with a gradual ascent up the far slope to a shoulder. Here Steeple comes more into view, out to the left and connected to Scoat Fell by a narrow neck of land. About 20 paces before reaching a prominent cairn at the top of the *rise* to Scoat Fell (not the top of Scoat Fell) you get the most terrific view of Black Crag and Pillar seen across Mirk Cove; this must be one of the finest views in the Lake District.

Turn left here for Steeple; the cairn marks where the narrow path runs out across the neck to this fine pointed peak and when you get there you see more of the fine cliffs of Black Crag filling the gap between Scoat Fell and Pillar: another tremendous view. You will leave Steeple with reluctance, but there is still a long way to go.

Return to the main ridge and continue east for a further 150 paces and the summit cairn of Scoat Fell will be found, appropriately, on the highest point of the fell which, in this case, happens to be the top of the wall traversing it. In a further 50 paces the wall ends in a tumble of huge boulders on the edge of a downfall.

Red Pike is now to the south-east, a sloping plateau ending in a dramatic escarpment tumbling down to Mosedale and looking across it to Lingmell and the Scafells. To reach it, it is easiest to pick a way down the boulders towards Pillar until you reach grass and then a narrow grooved path veers right and rises towards Red Pike. When this forks, unless you are in a tearing hurry and absolutely must bypass the summit by staying on the lower path, keep left and you will reach the very edge of the precipice, passing a subsidiary top and then continuing along it to reach the summit cairn, which is in a spectacular position on the highest rocks above the profound drop to Mosedale. It is a grand spot to rest quietly for a few moments, but no place to fool around.

Turning south along the rim a path declines gently on grass for about 600 paces and then, immediately before reaching a rash of boulders and rocks, turns left downhill. In so doing, it avoids a subsidiary summit marked by a large cairn (AW's Point 2629, OS spot height 801m), which is worth visiting for an interesting view back to the main summit, but also because you are then only about a hundred bouldery paces north of The Chair, a stone seat built from substantial rock slabs. When seated in it, you will be looking directly to Yewbarrow and, on the other side of Wastwater, Burnmoor Tarn. Low Tarn is on your right, but you will have to stand up and turn around to see Scoat Tarn. Return to the cairn (to outflank steep rocks) to regain the path heading towards Yewbarrow. There is a grassy section midway and then it steepens and leads down much rockier ground towards the hause of Dore Head.

On the descent you will have a clear view of Stirrup Crag which must be climbed to reach Yewbarrow, the final top. A belt of rocks near the top look distinctly intimidating, while a curved finger of rock on the left of the nose looks like a witch's fingernail beckoning you to some awful doom. Yet that is the way now: you can see a path and it struggles up some scree and then up slabby rocks and onto a shoulder before heading straight for the rock belt above. A series of rock steps lead to a little chimney which is well supplied with large holds (avoidable to the left) and then some huffing and puffing up a rock staircase soon leads you to the top of this blunt nose. Just beyond' are two cairns, one built on a stone slab, and although neither marks the top of the fell they do mark the real end of the uphill work, if not the difficulties, on this walk.

A slight descent to a depression is followed by a gentle rise to reach the summit cairn of Yewbarrow just over half a mile away. Then delightful walking over grass and around

Stirrup Crag on Yewbarrow, seen from the Red Pike path.

outcrops leads to where the spine of the fell starts to bend towards Wastwater. The ridge dips slightly before rising to end in the steep rocks of Bell Rib and it is from this dip the path leads into a stony gully which descends steeply to the right. (If you continue too far beyond the dip, you will soon be on rock and will reach the deep notch of Great Door, with a view on both sides of the ridge, and should then retreat.) The gully has plenty of loose scree and is therefore not particularly pleasant but the way soon reaches easier ground and descends beside the buttresses of Dropping Crag on the right, becoming a good path slanting down the fellside to reach a solid wall running down the last part of the ridge. Here you either cross by a ladder-stile and descend, or stay on the north side and use a gate at the foot of the ridge, then the path leads directly back to the car park. If you felt as I did when you get here, you will be fairly knackered but will have wonderful memories of a glorious day.

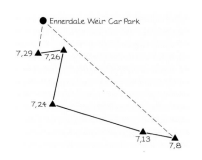

Ennerdale Weir Car Park

7,29 ▲ 7,26▲

7,24 ▲

7,13 ▲ ▲ 7,8

25 THE ENNERDALE SOUTHERN TOPS CIRCUIT

BEST MAP: *OS 1:25 000 Outdoor Leisure 4, North Western area*
APPROXIMATE TIME: *6 hours*
TERRAIN: *On good, if stony, paths for the approach, easier ground along the highest part of the summit ridge and some rough land with only faint paths in the final stages.*

ITINERARY	Book & Fell No	Height of ascent	Distance of ascent	Cumulative distance	Height above sea level	
		feet	miles	miles	feet	mtrs
ENNERDALE WEIR CAR PARK					330	101
Haycock	7.08	2350	5.75	5.75	2618	797
Caw Fell	7.13	120	1.00	6.75	2288	697
Lank Rigg	7.24	700	3.75	10.50	1775	541
Crag Fell	7.26	670	2.00	12.50	1710	523
Grike	7.29	150	1.00	13.50	1596	488
ENNERDALE WEIR CAR PARK				1.50	15.00	330	101
Totals of heights and distances of ascent		3990	15.00			

Mostly lower in altitude than the greater peaks of the Pillar group further south and grassy rather than rocky, the fells covered in this circuit nevertheless give a most interesting day's walking. Anybody ticking off 'Wainwrights' will find it particularly useful although I should mention that the ridge-line map does not give a connection between Caw Fell and Lank Rigg.

The start is the Forestry Commission's free car park at the western end of Ennerdale Water (grid ref 085154) reached from the village of Ennerdale Bridge. From here, walk south across the river bridge and then turn left (east) along the bank to join a broad track leading to the weir at the outflow from the lake. A public footpath between wire fences now shadows the south bank for about 100 yards to reach a kissing-gate almost on the shore. There is a National Trust sign here reading 'Anglers' Crag' and steep slopes of grass and scree are capped by a line of crags above, but these are part of Revelin Crag; Anglers' Crag is the one whose profile is seen ahead on the skyline, just above lake level. The

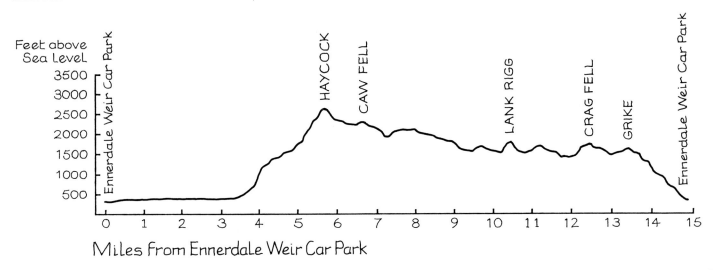

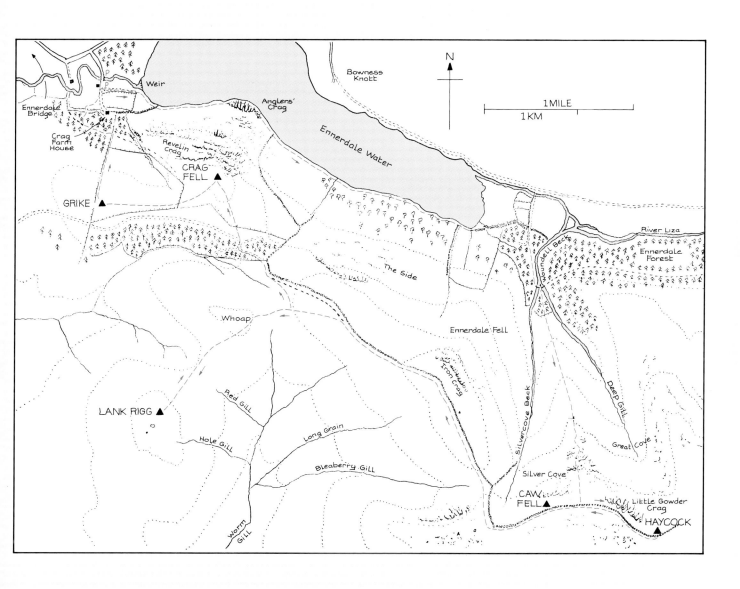

path towards it, which is a good if stony one, sticks close to the water's edge and while striding along it you have a good view across the lake to the seamed face of Herdus overlooking the craggy Bowness Knott.

Reaching the steep rocks of Anglers' Crag, the path leads by the water's edge towards a little grass-topped rocky headland called Robin Hood's Chair; it is a name that will strike a chord of recognition with walkers on Wainwright's Coast to Coast Walk, which also comes this way and which ends at Robin Hood's Bay on the Yorkshire coast. But beyond the Chair the rocks of Anglers' Crag drop sheer into the lake, so just before reaching it the path slants upwards for about 100ft to a fine perch and a good view up Ennerdale, then, once round the corner, it undulates across a scree slope and trends down again until it is once more just above water-level. A few Herdwick sheep graze peacefully in the shelter of the birch and oak trees that have colonised the lower slopes of The Side, but the path now has to pick an uncomfortable way over roots and through rocks along the bank to the head of the lake. Stiles, gates and signs take you on a broad grassy path along the northern edge of a large plantation to one more stile with a gravel track on its far side. Turning right along this leads immediately to a gate and into the timber, heading south. In about 150 yards, when the gravel track swings right, an obvious path leads up the right bank of Woundell Beck, marked by posts having a single blue-painted circle cut into them.

At the point where Silvercove Beck joins Woundell Beck, a good footbridge (AW's greasy plank is no longer there) leads onto the narrow tongue of land between Silvercove Beck and Deep Gill and here you turn uphill on a carpet of larch needles, heading for Haycock. The trees do crowd closely on the path but there is no danger of the way not being clear enough and the forest edge is soon reached, where a stile over the fence leads to a good path winding up a broad and heather-covered ridge. About half way up this ridge the path kinks to the left but quickly realises its mistake and soon rejoins the broad crest to reach a substantial cairn. This could be the one shown by the OS on the 500-metre contour, but there is another cairn higher up on the next rise, so it is difficult to be sure. By the time you have reached this second one, you will be above the heather zone and rising up grass slopes towards rock outcrops ahead. The rocks add greatly to the interest of the latter part of the ascent but then they merge into easier-angled grass gradients leading directly to the wall marching along the top of the ridge.

Looking left from here, the rocky outcrop of Little Gowder Crag interrupts the rise but an obvious path beside the wall quickly skirts it and then curves over rocky ground to the higher summit of Haycock with its two cairns, one on each side of the wall. It is quite a good viewpoint to the higher fells in the east but, of more importance today, looking west all the remaining fells on the circuit can be seen from above.

The next top is Caw Fell and from this vantage point on Haycock you will appreciate the truth of AW's comment that 'From no point of view does the fell look like anything

Ennerdale Water and Crag Fell seen over Little Gowder Crag from Haycock.

other than a broadly-buttressed sprawling uncorseted graceless lump with a vast flattened summit similarly devoid of a single distinguishing landmark.' Poor Caw Fell! Retracing steps down the rocky slope past little Gowder Crag, stay beside the wall to reach the top, but apart from the wall, the only landmark is the cairn, and you will have to cross the wall to find that, for both wall and adjacent path ignore it as they head west. (It is worth mentioning that the top of Caw Fell is in fact $\frac{3}{4}$ mile east of the name 'Caw Fell' on the OS map.) The wall is a perfect guide as it turns north and descends fairly steeply on grass to a col at the head of Silvercove Beck then rises beyond it, past a cairn on Ennerdale Fell, above the unseen Iron Crag. Crag Fell is ahead, further along the continuation of the ridge, but you will not get a better opportunity than this to visit Lank Rigg, another AW top which is clearly visible across the wide bowl drained by Worm Gill. A beeline towards it would involve too much loss of height and the only realistic way to reach it is to veer westwards away from the wall towards the intervening grassy hump of Whoap and this will be over pathless ground unless you spot a tractor track leading to the juicy col before the gentle rise towards its top. The track leads over a shoulder but then curves away towards the solitary boulder that appears to mark the summit. Lank Rigg is, however, to the south-west, so the track must be abandoned and a pathless stretch of grass has to be crossed before a faint trod develops on the descent to a narrow neck linking Lank Rigg to Whoap.

As I paused here to consider both the climb ahead and that I would have it all to reverse shortly, I will admit to thinking that I wished AW hadn't bothered with this fell at all. Lank Rigg is where he hid a two-bob coin under a flat stone four feet from the trig point, calling it 'buried treasure', and invited visitors to search for it. The coin was clearly an inducement to visit the damned fell – and when you too are facing this un-welcome climb you will probably share my feelings. Then I thought: 'Well, if Wainwright could be bothered to write it up, I had better climb it and stop moaning.' In fact, when you do get there you will find a little cairn about 5ft away from the trig point and a surprisingly good view. AW thought it 'unremarkable' (another reason why he left his two-bob?) but I thought the views were extensive and that the ascent had, after all, been worth the effort. There is not much joy, however, in walking over to the other cairn, beyond a little tarn in a depression, for the view to the west is dominated by the cooling towers of Sellafield.

Crag Fell comes next and it is visible to the north, but you must first reverse steps to Whoap and then, beyond it, head down a trackless grass slope towards a junction of the ridge-top wall and a forestry plantation. The current OS map is out of date here and you will now find a gate and a stile to a forest track; turn left along this but then curve right and uphill to meet another track. Turn left again, but only for 50 yards to where a cairn marks a narrow path heading north-west up a clearing. The forest fence is crossed by a stile and the path then leads up more open grassy ground to the top of Crag Fell, which is marked by a pile of stones on a rocky outcrop. Again, AW didn't rate the view very highly and grumbled about Calder Hall (Sellafield) and the forestry but Ennerdale Water is visible and I thought it was a grand, if distant, view to Pillar, Brandreth and Haystacks.

The last top is Grike, seen a mile away directly across a depression to the west, but the best way there is to turn south-west and pick a way down the rough and mostly pathless slopes of Crag Fell to reach a stile over a wire fence which runs parallel to the old mine road. A path now shadows this fence and although it splashes over some soggy ground en route it leads directly to a large cairn and two large windbreaks on the windy top of Grike. By the time I got there the light was beginning to fade (it was early January) but I had no difficulty in seeing the wire fence only 50 yards to the west of the summit. It led in a very direct line towards the outflow from Ennerdale Water and there were traces of a path beside it, so it was obviously the way to go. The way becomes

Lank Rigg seen from Caw Fell.

steeper as it descends beside the plantation on the lower slopes, then reaches a gate and stile, where you turn left on a slanting track into the forest. After a short way, a sharper descent down a firebreak on the right leads to a track at the foot of the slope and a right turn along it would lead directly to Crag Farm House. In only 50 yards, however, a gate on the left enables you to bypass the farm and slant across to join the main track back to the car park. It ends a grand day.

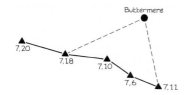

26 THE COMPLETE HIGH STILE RIDGE

BEST MAP: *OS 1:25 000 Outdoor Leisure 4, North Western area*
APPROXIMATE TIME: *7 hours*
TERRAIN: *Some untracked ground (mostly over grass) in the early stages of the climb to the ridge and vaguely defined paths on the highest stony ground, but the going is not generally difficult.*

ITINERARY	Book & Fell No	Height of ascent	Distance of ascent	Cumulative distance	Height above sea level	
		feet	miles	miles	feet	mtrs
BUTTERMERE					300	91
Starling Dodd	7.18	1800	3.25	3.25	2085	633
Great Borne	7.20	420	1.50	4.75	2019	616
Starling Dodd	7.18	480	1.50	6.25	2085	633
Red Pike (Buttermere)	7.10	650	1.25	7.50	2479	755
High Stile	7.06	350	0.75	8.25	2644	806
High Crag	7.11	80	1.00	9.25	2443	744
BUTTERMERE			2.50	11.75	300	91
Totals of heights and distances of ascent		3780	11.75			

The long ridge of high land separating Ennerdale from Buttermere is uniformly dull on its Ennerdale flanks and largely given over to conifer plantations, but the northern slopes are as exciting as the southern ones are boring. Here the retreating ice took great bites from the ridge, exposing sharp-edged glacial combes buttressed by fine crags where ravens soar. This is classic fellwalking country.

The best part of the ridge is, without doubt, the stretch between Red Pike and High Crag, but there is more to the ridge than that for it stretches east from Red Pike over the other two Wainwright tops of Starling Dodd and Great Borne. As mentioned in the Introduction, very strong walkers could make a circuit of the entire Ennerdale skyline, on both sides of the valley and starting at Great Borne, but will need 13–15 hours to do it. I suspect that most fellwalkers want an enjoyable day rather than a marathon. This walk, therefore, links all the tops on this part of the AW ridge-line, but with Great Borne

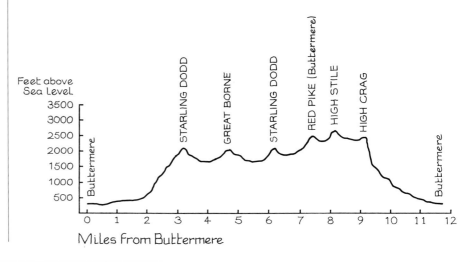

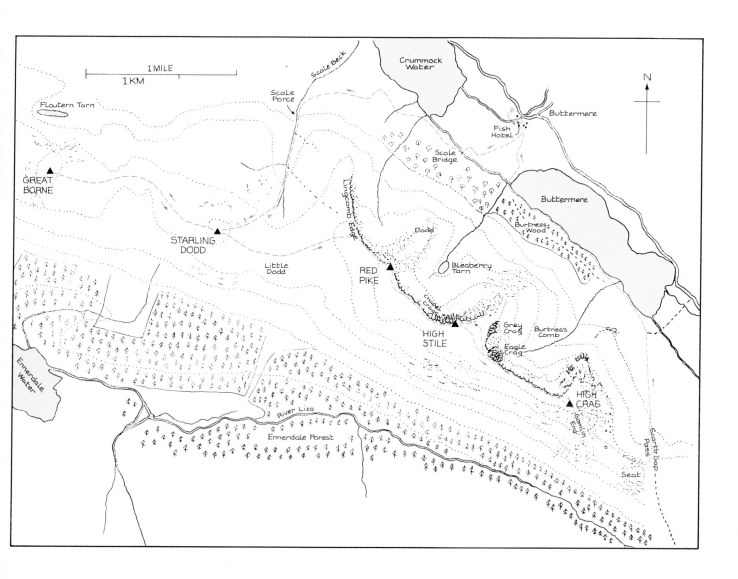

GREAT BORNE

Floutern Tarn

Scale Force

Scale Beck

Crummock Water

Fish Hotel

Buttermere

Scale Bridge

STARLING DODD

Little Dodd

Lingcomb Edge

Dodd

Bleaberry Tarn

Burtness Wood

Buttermere

RED PIKE

Chapel Crags

HIGH STILE

Grey Crag

Burtness Comb

Eagle Crag

Ennerdale Water

River Liza

Ennerdale Forest

HIGH CRAG

Gamlin End

Scarth Gap Pass

Seat

1 MILE

1 KM

N

included as an extension from Starling Dodd especially for those walkers who have not yet been there or who may be 'Wainwright-bagging'.

The best place to start is Buttermere village where there is a large car park near the Fish Hotel. The charge there is now £3–00 per day so I am not too surprised that many motorists park on the roadside. A level bridleway next to the hotel, signed for Scale Bridge and Scale Force, leads towards Buttermere lake, but when it forks veer to the right (south-west) along a frequently muddy track edged with blackthorn and overlooked by the oak-covered slopes sweeping down from Red Pike. The track turns right just before reaching Scale Bridge and for a short way runs beside the beck, whose shallow waters are of a crystal clarity enhanced by the tresses of green weed that waver delicately in the currents.

Having crossed the bridge and turned right, a stony path now picks a way over the fellside to the north-east, rising gently, with marshy land colonised by osiers and alders stretching down to the shores of Crummock Water on the right. When the line of cairns marking the way turns sharply left uphill do not ignore them, for to continue straight ahead leads into some exceptionally juicy ground (for which AW recommended thigh-length gumboots as the ideal wear). Even the preferred way involves balletic leaping from boulder to boulder but you stand a better chance of keeping your feet dry. Still rising, the path swings further west into a wide basin, on the left of which is the tree-filled gill of Scale Beck and Lakeland's highest waterfall, Scale Force. If you are there when the trees are leafless, you may see something of the long slender ribbon of the cascade, but normally vegetation obscures the view, even from the footbridge over the beck directly beneath the falls.

Do not cross the footbridge; the path beyond leads over some of the wettest, squelchiest bog imaginable towards Floutern Tarn, which is why that possible approach to Great Borne is to be avoided like the plague. Instead, turn up the excellent man-made stone staircase on the left bank of the gill and follow it as it climbs steeply. You will have to be content with the thunderous roar of the waters for you will get little sight of them until almost at the top of the rise, when a final 20-ft cascade becomes visible. About 200 yards above this upper part of the waterfall a path in a deep trench cuts into the heather and heads up the steep slope on the left, but ignore it; also ignore the next, in a further 350 yards or so and marked by a cairn. Instead continue (despite your misgivings at the lack of a path) up the course of the beck towards its headwaters. When the stream forks, head right and you will soon reach a large three-chambered sheepfold. Now bilberry and then grass slopes with a few boulders lead to the rounded grass-and-gravel top of Starling Dodd where a large summit cairn bristles with old iron fence posts. That is the hardest part of the day over. The views are nothing to get excited about; I took numerous photographs on my last visit but there are far better landscapes to follow in due course.

Looking down Scale Beck, with Grasmoor beyond.

Great Borne is 1½ miles WNW and even from Starling Dodd it can be seen that its top is a mass of embedded grey stones surrounded by heather. Fortunately it is easy going over grass to the intervening depression and then a rise of just under 400ft to reach the huge cairn (this north top was a favourite viewing point for our Victorian forbears, although Heaven alone knows why), the trig point on the nearby south top, and the windbreak. You've been there, done that, but there's no T-shirt, so all there is now to do is to toddle back to Starling Dodd and get on with the real business of this fine ridge.

Easy grass slopes lead from Starling Dodd down to the depression at the head of Scale

Beck, rise almost imperceptibly over the mini-mound of Little Dodd and then a path develops beside a line of old fence posts rising to the north-east. This path swings right to shadow the posts on the rise towards Red Pike but, by allowing your course to drift further left you will soon get a grand view down to the Buttermere valley and back along the curve of Lingcomb Edge, with Crummock Water and Mellbreak in the view. The path then continues up shaly red scree to reach the top of Red Pike, where a semi-circular windbreak also functions as the summit cairn. Again the views are splendid and the ruddy colouring in the shales and rocks, especially visible towards the subsidiary top of Dodd, add to the appeal. But better is still to come.

From Red Pike a good path, marked by an occasional fence post, curves round the rim of the combe towards High Stile, the view ahead being dominated by the deep-cut gullies and shattered rocks of Chapel Crags which fringe it. A glance below on the left reveals Bleaberry Tarn, cupped in what is apparently believed to be the crater of an extinct volcano, with Buttermere village seen beyond and far below. Then the path climbs once more, scrambling easily to the right of the upper buttresses of Chapel Crags to reach a cairn on a rock platform on their highest point. If this is not the top of High Stile it ought to be: the fact that the OS show another spot height one miserable metre higher (where there is another cairn) about 250 yards to the east cannot detract from the superb position of *this* one: five paces from it and you are standing right on the edge of the sheer drop overlooking Bleaberry Tarn. This viewpoint (which AW treated as the top) is where you will linger; reaching the other cairn (that is, if you can be bothered) is just a formality.

The summit area of High Stile is very rocky, paths are consequently not well marked and other cairns may prove misleading. For example, a line of them deceptively continues around the rim of the combe, swinging to the north-east and descending a little to reach a very prominent cairn on the north-east spur; it is another good viewpoint, but not the way to continue along the ridge top to High Crag. Fortunately a few iron fence posts (and one, set into a large block, is especially prominent) point the way across this stony ground to the south-east and then, although the posts continue, the path becomes more obvious as it descends much less stony ground and follows the rim of Burtness (or Birkness) Comb. The fine rocks of Grey Crag and Eagle Crag both buttress the ridge here and although you are unlikely to see any climbers on the latter (since its main faces are out of sight from here), you may well see some on Grey Crag's upper rocks. There is also a particularly fine view across the comb to Fleetwith Pike beyond the stretch to High Crag, which now follows.

The top of High Crag is reached after some slight depressions in the narrow crest of the ridge and at the end of a short rise, passing first one large cairn and then, in five yards another; they both looked the same height to me. The ground slopes away in all directions but drops steeply beyond the second cairn, with striking views to the head of

Looking over Bleaberry Tarn to Red Pike and Mellbreak from High Stile.

Ennerdale and towards the rumpled, crumpled top of Haystacks, seen beyond the intervening minor top of Seat.

That steep drop is Gamlin End and although AW describes the descent being guided by the fence posts (not much sign of any now) I remember it as a scree run thirty years ago. Then it deteriorated into a dreadful mess on which you were quite likely to go arse-over-tip as you tried to sneak down it. Happily, it is now much improved and a pleasant zigzag path goes down the upper part, then traverses out right before working back left and down towards a small pool on the depression below. The rugged little top of Seat rises immediately beyond it and gives the last short climb of the day.

The descent from Seat also used to be a nasty business, slithering down a mixture of rock slabs, rubble and scree towards Scarth Gap below, but that grand team of lads financed by the National Trust (and whom I met at work on the Black Sail Pass) have created a splendid pitched path winding down the rough ground. It's a vast improvement – almost a doddle, in fact.

The descent towards Buttermere that now follows, down the Scarth Gap Pass, is very straightforward but very stony in its upper part; some of those sharp rocks are real ankle-crackers. Then the path runs out onto a shelf and you slither along on little stones like ball-bearings for a while until it gets rougher again on the last descent. Now trend left to take the path along the margin of this beautiful lake. Just before reaching Burtness Wood, the track forks and a permissive path stays close to the lake shore, allowing more delightful views across the water, before a footbridge and gates at the north-west corner of the lake lead to the final stroll back to Buttermere village.

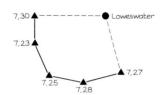

27 THE LOWESWATER SKYLINE

BEST MAP: *OS 1:25 000 Outdoor Leisure 4, North Western area*
APPROXIMATE TIME: *6 hours*
TERRAIN: *A mixture of good paths over firm ground, some open grassy fell and some boggy stretches to be crossed.*

ITINERARY	Book & Fell No	Height of ascent	Distance of ascent	Cumulative distance	Height above sea level	
		feet	miles	miles	feet	mtrs
LOWESWATER					400	122
Burnbank Fell	7.30	1250	3.00	3.00	1580	482
Blake Fell	7.23	420	1.00	4.00	1878	573
Gavel Fell	7.25	270	1.00	5.00	1720	526
Hen Comb	7.28	775	1.00	6.00	1661	509
Mellbreak	7.27	1000	1.25	7.25	1676	512
LOWESWATER			2.00	9.25	400	122
Totals of heights and distances of ascent		3715	9.25			

The ridge-line map links Burnbank Fell, Blake Fell and Gavel Fell. But when you stand on top of Gavel Fell and consider that you have to return to Loweswater, somehow, you soon realise that Hen Comb and Mellbreak, which are both Wainwright tops but have no ridge connections and indeed are separated by substantial depressions, are nevertheless close enough to be included in a single circuit. Apart from anything else, Mellbreak is itself a ridge in its own right, with two linked tops more than half a mile apart and with a fine spur leading back almost directly to Loweswater. I have therefore linked these five fells (which are all 'Wainwright tops') in this walk. Apart from ticking these off if you are so inclined, you will enjoy some excellent views of the Buttermere fells as you go. An escape could be made back to Loweswater after Gavel Fell, or after Hen Comb, if the legs are protesting.

    AW started his ascent of Burnbank Fell from Waterend, at the north end of Loweswater, but with the two additional fells added I suggest it is better to start from the

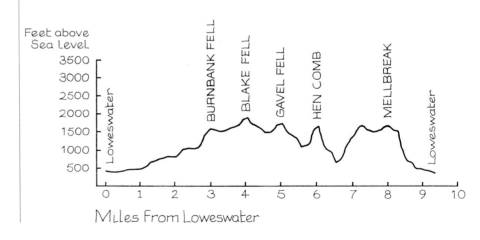

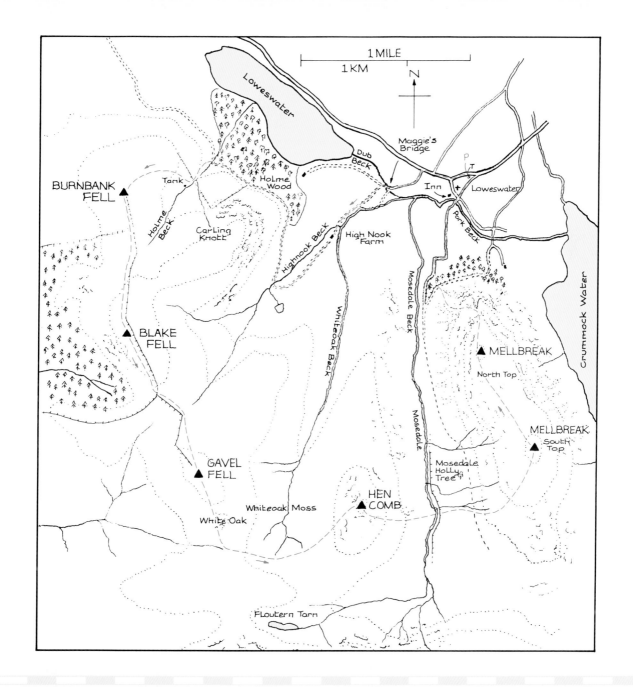

On Blake Fell, looking south-east, with a panorama of (left to right): Dale Head, Fleetwith Pike, the High Stile ridge and Pillar above Ennerdale.

southern end of Loweswater (or the hamlet itself). This will both avoid any tarmac-bashing and also enable you to enjoy a fine terrace walk overlooking Holme Wood. Parking is admittedly less easy at the southern end of the lake but there is room for several cars next to the public telephone box (grid ref 143212) or at a car park at Maggie's Bridge (grid ref 135210). If you start from the telephone box, follow the road westwards and then turn down the second metalled road on the left, which leads to Maggie's Bridge. Here Dub Beck, the outlet from Loweswater, is crossed – and the car park is just beyond the bridge on the right. From here turn up the track signed to High Nook Farm, go through the yard and carry on, with Highnook Beck now on your right, to a gate at an intake wall. About 300 yards beyond this, swing right to cross a footbridge over the stream and then a wide grass track slants gently uphill to the north and contours below Carling Knott and just above Holme Wood. This is a delightful and easy ramble and you should store up happy feelings as you walk along it, for what follows next is sheer hard work.

The track kinks into the gill of Holme Beck and as soon as you have crossed the footbridge you should leave the track and follow a thin path up the gill, crossing the low fence (which is down in many places anyway) and then, before reaching a water-tank, turn uphill. This is the hard work: a pathless, steep grass slope. You won't have enough breath to whistle but you might manage to hum a tune with a regular beat that will encourage you to keep putting one foot in front of the other as you toil upwards; I find 'Onward, Christian Soldiers' works quite well. Done this way, the slope is soon conquered and you can turn south-west along the very broad ridge to reach what can only be called the highest place, for it is hardly a point, where there is a small cairn in acres of grass. Next to it is a rusty iron straining post, its top draped with other bits of twisted iron fencing, a weird mountain totem-pole. This is Burnbank Fell; it is not very exciting and the views are not much to write home about, but take heart, for everything starts to get better from here on. Well, almost here.

A wire fence leads due south towards the eminence of Blake Fell, seen rising ahead over a grassy prairie, and a footpath runs beside the fence. It soon reaches a transverse fence which is crossed by a stile but, unlike almost all other stiles which are built next to a post so you have something to hold onto, this one is between posts so that you only have a wobbly wire to catch hold of, with some risk of damage to the family jewels. Once over, the path on the other side leads, with no further obstacles, over heather to the top of Blake Fell. There is a largely complete stone windbreak here which I imagine must have been fashioned from the original summit cairn, and unless you crouch in the lee of a peat grough just below the top, it is virtually the only shelter on these open heights. Take advantage of it, therefore, to stop and recuperate. It is also a superb viewpoint for the Buttermere and Grasmoor fells and you could sit here for a long time watching clouds and sunlight painting the landscape with shadows.

Looking to Robinson over Crummock Water from the north ridge of Mellbreak.

Leaving the top of Blake Fell, I was not aware of any signs of the ring-fencing of the summit area that AW groused about so much in the Pictorial Guide, and had no difficulty following the path beside the fence to the SSE towards Gavel Fell. It descends gently to a depression where there is a proper stile to step over, which also enables you to avoid paddling through a bog, and then rises beside the fence until this ends just before reaching the summit. The cairn on the grassy top has several rubbing-stones nearby (normally used by sheep, rarely by people) suggesting that it was previously bigger than it is now.

A long descent follows, south-east but soon swinging east, towards the obvious and isolated hill of Hen Comb. The slope steepens lower down and then runs out onto a very broad, very boggy, very wet hause (Whiteoak Moss) which has to be crossed somehow as there is no way of dodging it, and then firmer ground allows a much pleasanter climb towards the top of the hill ahead. As I climbed this, a dense white cloud could be seen rushing towards me and I was soon enveloped in a fierce hail storm with high winds and stinging ice-lumps battering me. My two little dogs, despite being partially protected by the coats that I had made for them some time ago, rushed around trying to hide their faces from the onslaught, but as I reached the top the hail ceased and the fells were bathed in sunlight again. AW says that this is the sort of fell that is 'sometimes climbed, but rarely twice', but the views I enjoyed that day from Hen Comb, especially towards Grasmoor, will linger long with me and I sat near the large cairn for quite a few minutes, and not just because I was knackered.

Another long, grassy and pathless descent follows from here towards Mosedale (which is, of course, only one of the several Mosedales in the Lake District), with a good view of the Mosedale Holly Tree, the only *single* tree to be named by the OS on their maps (the 'Borrowdale Yews' are also named, but there are four of them). The depression is not so wide as Whiteoak Moss but it is nearly as wet and you must jump over Mosedale Beck (fortunately it is only a cock-stride) and then cross a low wire fence on the far side before the last ascent can begin. There is no path up the slope, nor would you expect one I think, and so it is a steady climb up grass slopes, with the angle mercifully easing as you gain height and swing north-east to a cairn in the area of the south top of Mellbreak, which the OS rather irritatingly show to be 10ft higher than the north top.

There is a surprisingly wide and comparatively deep depression between the two tops, but a well-used path over grassy, peaty and then heathery ground links them without difficulty. The cairn on the north top is built on a fine rock plinth thrusting out of heather, a much more appropriate summit for such a distinctive mountain than the south top. Although the views from here, particularly towards Grasmoor and the other Buttermere fells, are arresting, the descent down the north ridge which now follows shows them to greater effect and also presents a delightful aerial view of the pastoral lands around Loweswater.

The route is well-trodden, down heathery grooves to a first shoulder (which is a good viewpoint), down a steeper step or rib where rock is exposed and with an awkward bit where the gully is being eroded. The path then runs out onto a scree slope which leads to a last gentle decline over grass towards a small plantation. The path cuts through this and a gate gives access to a walled lane which wiggles downhill to cross Park Beck; a left turn here up the slope on the other side leads directly to the hospitable Kirkstile Inn, a splendid place for a bite of something and a drink before rejoining the car.

INDEX

Fell names in CAPITALS are the subjects of chapters in Wainwright's *Pictorial Guides to the Lakeland Fells*

Page numbers in *italics* refer to illustrations